THE DARK PEOPLES

OF

THE LAND OF SUNSHINE.

THE
DARK PEOPLES

OF

THE LAND OF SUNSHINE

*A POPULAR ACCOUNT
OF THE PEOPLES AND TRIBES OF AFRICA,*

THEIR PHYSICAL CHARACTERS, MANNERS, AND CUSTOMS.

BY

G. T. BETTANY, M.A., B.Sc.

With many Illustrations.

WARD, LOCK AND CO.,
LONDON, NEW YORK, AND MELBOURNE.
1890.
Reprinted by Mnemosyne Publishing Co., Inc. Miami, Florida

INTRODUCTION.

FAR less than Europe and Asia has Africa been
famous in ancient history. Egypt with its massive pyramids and temples and cities, Carthage with its
naval power and foreign conquests, Abyssinia with its
early Arab, Jewish, and Egyptian relations, have alone
afforded material of great import in the early story of the
nations; but these largely, if not entirely, derived their
cultivation from Asia. Many facts point to Africa as
having received human inhabitants later than Asia,
though yet long previous to historic records. The climate,
the extent of deserts and forest land, the great lake sys-
tems of the interior, with their extremely variable floods,
the abundance of snakes, crocodiles, hippopotamuses,
rhinoceroses, lions, and other opponents of man, all combined to render the advance of the human army slow,
and only to be accomplished after long seasoning and
much adaptation to the conditions. The procuring of
food was one of the least difficulties in many regions;
dates, bananas, and other bountifully abundant products
of nature rendered life easily supported. Of the dangers
to life from animals, malaria, floods and deserts, some
could be combated, but not at first, if even now, upon
equal terms; others are insidious or sudden, and against
them the dark inhabitants could do but little. We must

probably view the north-east of Africa as receiving successive invasions of the early inhabitants of south-west Asia, who developed and varied in those lands, and gradually gave off branches towards the fertile regions of the south. In doing so they became modified, and it is possible that the Hottentots and Bushmen are the degenerate survivors of some of the earliest races, who gradually reached the extreme south of the continent. Had the country been as favourable to mankind on the whole as India and China, we might have met with a vastly larger population in Africa than is to be found there. But man found his instinct to compete with his brother man, to struggle with him for valued possessions or for food, so echoed by nature in this equatorial continent, that it overcame the tropical tendency to sloth as nothing else could have done; and such civilisation as Central Africa has attained is greatly due to the perpetual contests in which the more cunningly led, or the more robust, gained the day. And even now it is probable that the part of war in the elevation of the African is by no means over, however we may deplore the savagery and misery of the process.

No doubt war has been largely accompanied by slavery, and now-a-days slavery has its chief seat in Africa. From time immemorial, captured African women and children, and to a less extent men, have been made the slaves of the conquerors, though not always ill-treated; and it was by no means the introduction of a new system when the Portuguese took slaves from Angola in the fifteenth, and Sir John Hawkins from the coast of Guinea in the sixteenth century. The evil, the shame, was that civilised Christian nations could tolerate or foster traffic in human lives as property. Although European nations now discourage what once they favoured, it is not doubtful that they are still insufficiently energetic in putting down the exit of slaves from Africa, upon which depends the profit of the trade now carried on chiefly by Arabs. This people has hitherto had more influence on Africa than Europeans, partly, no doubt, because the Arabs are far better adapted to the climate of Africa, and partly because they have more cunningly and unscrupulously laid themselves out to take advantage of and play upon the evil side of the African nature. They have appeared as traders, introducing many of the articles which the Africans most want, and buying therewith the ivory and the slaves for which outside nations will give them high prices. They do not object to becoming petty conquerors or raiders for slaves, and they get their human property to carry the burden of their non-living purchases in the long marches to the coast. Thus vast regions of Central Africa are dotted over with the camps of Arab traders and raiders, who are centres of confusion and death. But no word-pictures can paint with sufficient power the dark scenes of these journeys to the coast, of the cruelties and the sufferings they occasion. The fact that the tracks can often be sufficiently made out by the bones of dead slaves which lie alongside them, will indicate the proportions to which the curse of Africa extends, and the duty of all Christian nations is evidently to combine to make such a state of things cease.

Ancient Egypt, the rival of China in antiquity of civilisation, has left remains which fascinate and interest us even more than the modern population. We seem never to be at the end of the charm and the contrast of the old with the new life. Conquerors, artists, builders, architects, religionists to an extreme, the Egyptians not only filled their land with most lasting monuments, but their influence radiated far, both in Asia and in Europe. Unquestionably the ancients achieved marvellous results, but they were mostly for the aggrandisement of rulers, and cost the blood of hundreds of thousands of slaves. The smallest result of willing modern co-operation is a more noble achievement. Carthage, like Egypt, won great victories, spread her dominion far over the globe, and came near to humbling the pride of Rome ; but she went down more irretrievably than Egypt, and we know far less of her than is to be desired. Abyssinia, early notable as a refuge of Judaism and of early Christianity, has continued at various dates and in various ways to claim and gain the notice of Europe. The late kings Theodore and Johannes were almost equally successful in this direction, though for opposite reasons.

From the spread of Christianity onwards, Africa has played a more and more important part in the world's history. From Alexandria and North Africa proceeded many a discourse and treatise ; and in them many a controversy was decided, many an act of discipline was exercised, which had an influence far and wide over the Christian Church. Later on the fierce propaganda of the Mahometans spread rapidly over the north of the continent, and the Saracen power established many Mahometan sultanates, until North-west Africa became a conquering centre from which Spain was overcome and Western civilisation was threatened. Yet again, in more modern times, a Moslem power, the Turkish, made North-west Africa its prey, and still retains the semblance of power.

But with the fifteenth century voyagers the turn of Europe began, and for four centuries Europeans have

A

been slowly gaining a hold on the dark continent. It has proved a most difficult task to master and influence these dark peoples, especially because the climate has proved so very deadly to Europeans in most parts of the continent. The lack of roads and the difficulties of rivers have made all travelling hazardous, and the impossibility of being certain that the negro ruler who welcomed the stranger one day, would not kill or expel him the next, has added greatly to the obstacles to opening up the continent to European enterprise. The more temperate climes of the south have been much more open to settlers, but even here the suspicions of the natives, the want of consideration or generosity of the intruders, and the inevitable misunderstandings between the two have brought about frequent wars, and in many ways greatly lowered the character of the natives. The European has conferred on the South Africans the doubtful gifts of gunpowder and guns, and the still more disastrous fiery spirits and devastating diseases; and even if the same energy were displayed in bestowing upon them benefits worthy of acceptance, and in setting before them the example of a good life, we fear that nothing will avail to prevent the extinction of many tribes. Possibly others will survive as a labouring class under European masters. Madagascar is, on the whole, in a more hopeful state than a great part of Africa. The Malay invaders, who constitute a great part of the people, have a bright and very capable intellect; and this great island may possibly become the Japan of Africa.

Manifold reasons have thus been given why the study of Africa ought to gain the attention of every philanthropist, of every student of mankind, of every politician, of every one who feels that he is born in advantageous circumstances, and may find it possible to help in civilising or elevating his less favoured fellow-creatures. This section of "The World's Inhabitants" appeals more powerfully even than Asia to the sympathies, the efforts, and the intelligent consideration of the English speaking peoples of the world.

CONTENTS.

CHAPTER		PAGE
I.	The Egyptians	1
II.	The Inhabitants of Northern Africa	20
III.	The Nubians and Abyssinians	44
IV.	The Gallas, Somalis, etc.	64
V.	The Waganda and the Eastern Soudanese	73
VI.	The Central Soudanese	106
VII.	The Western Africans from the Senegal to the Ogoway	121
VIII.	The South Africans	151
IX.	South Tropical Africans	178
X.	The Malagasy	205

THE INHABITANTS OF AFRICA.

CHAPTER I.
The Egyptians.

Early civilisation—Menes—The great pyramids—The earliest papyrus—Egyptian conquests—The kings of Thebes—The Hyksos—Thothmes I.—Seti I.—Ramses II.—Exodus of the Israelites—Decline of Egypt—Conquest by the Persians—Later conquerors—Physical characters of ancient Egyptians—Dress—Egyptian religion—The priesthood—Egyptian architecture—Embalming and burial—The Book of the Dead—Language—Hieroglyphics—Arts and sciences—The modern Egyptians—Importance of the Nile—The fellahs—Egyptian women—Peasant's dress—Food—Character—The Copts—The upper classes—Habits — Dress of men — Dress of women—Children—Houses—Divorce and slavery—Religious pride—Fatalism—Habits and character.

UNLIKE Europe and Asia, Africa can boast of but two of the great peoples of former times, the Egyptians and the Carthaginians. It was the scene of many of the ravages and some of the glories of medieval Mahometanism; and it may now be described as the

B

theatre of a vast attempt on the part of Europeans to gain control and exercise influence, in the face of a determined Mahometan propagandism in the central regions.

Egypt, a fertile valley and a delta, all else desert, must have been very early inhabited; but prehistoric remains have not yet been discovered in great abundance. Such as have been found are of the neolithic or polished stone type. Undoubtedly the greater part of the delta has been formed since the civilisation of Egypt had reached considerable development. Whether this civilisa-

Early civilisation. tion was introduced into Egypt from abroad, or grew up there, it is impossible to say; but already in the earliest monuments, and in the time of the ancient empire, the Egyptians were a distinct race, long-headed, short and thick-set, with reddish-brown complexion, broad forehead, full nostrils, large mouth, and smooth hair, very unlike negroes or Arabs. Many students place the ancient Egyptians among the Caucasians, others include them among the Hàmitic peoples as a distinct type.

It is probable that the Egyptian is the oldest civilisation of which we have monumental records. How many thousands of years should be assigned to it is doubtful, but the medium estimate of Mariette dates the foundation of Memphis as B.C. 5004. After legendary dynasties

Menes. in which the gods and demigods were the kings, Menes appears as the first founder of a united kingdom, who extended his sway from This, in upper Egypt, northwards, and founded Memphis as his capital, near the Sphinx, probably built about his time, and at the apex of the Nile delta, part of which he reclaimed from the Nile by the great dyke of Kosheish.

With the fourth dynasty begins the great building era of ancient Egypt. Khufu (Cheops) built the great pyra-

The great pyramids. mid near Memphis, and his successors Khafra (Chephren) and Men-ka-ra, built its two companions. Many other splendid tombs of wealthy and powerful subjects have been preserved. The kings, wielding the manual labour of the poor as an implement made for themselves, exercised a compulsion which has left its relics down to our own day ; but it does not appear that wars were then frequent or exhaustive. In the fifth dynasty, assigned by Mariette to B.C. 3951-3703, the very ancient papyrus of Phah-hotep, son of the king Tat-ka-ra Assa, was written. It is the most ancient manuscript known to exist, though some inscriptions are older. The author refers to Osiris as god, but appears to have an idea of one god. His philosophy is of singular interest as showing how far the human soul had risen nearly six thousand years ago. The following is one passage quoted by Prof. Sayce: "If thou art become great after thou hast been lowly, and if thou hast heaped up riches after poverty, being because of that the chiefest in thy city; if thou art known for thy wealth and art become a great lord;—let not thy heart be puffed up because of thy riches, for it is God who has given them unto thee. Despise not another who is as thou wast; be towards him as towards thy equal." *The earliest papyrus.*

In the sixth dynasty the kings of Egypt became conquerors, attacking the south-eastern Asiatic peoples, and having many negroes in their armies from Ethiopia, which was already subject to the Egyptians. The dynasty ended with Queen Nitocris, who enlarged the third great pyramid, or that of Men-ka-ra. This queen has become the centre of many legends. After this there is a considerable gap in Egyptian history. The next records which are trustworthy describe the eleventh dynasty, about B.C. 3064, seated further south, at Thebes, and apparently signalising the domination of a different people. The obelisk of Heliopolis, near Cairo, the oldest known, the fixing of the southern boundary of Egypt at the fortresses of Semneh and Kunnuch, thirty-five miles south of the second cataract, the creation of Lake Mœris west of the Nile Delta for artificial irrigation, are among the conspicuous works of the twelfth dynasty, whose kings were principally called Amenenhat and Usertasen. In the sixth year of Usertasen II. a family of Semites arrived from the East, and begged permission to settle on the Nile. "We may still see them with their black hair and hooked *Egyptian conquests.* *The kings of Thebes.*

noses, and Phœnician garments of many colours, like the one which Joseph wore " (Sayce).   A succession of Semitic tribes followed them, and gradually the whole country came under their control.   Their kings are known as the

The Hyksos.   Hyksos, or Shepherd kings, who ruled for 500 years as the fifteenth, sixteenth, and seventeenth dynasties. They adopted Egyptian civilisation, and showed skill and power in their erection of monolithic

obelisks. It was probably during the period of the Shepherd kings that first Abraham and then Joseph came to Egypt. The Hyksos were finally expelled from the country, and the eighteenth dynasty, founded by Aahmes, rose on their ruin.

The eighteenth and nineteenth dynasties mark the greatest period of Egypt. Both from monuments and papyri we have many records which show the great progress in conquest and in arts which the Egyptians then made. Thothmes I. marched *Thothmes I.* through Phœnicia and Syria, and added the Soudan to Egypt. He began the great works of the temple of Amen-ra at Thebes, which his sister Hatshepu, or Hatasu, continued, and also set up the great obelisk of Karnak. Thothmes III., who reigned fifty-three years, waged prolonged wars in South-eastern Asia, in the course of which he captured Nineveh. Amenophis III. built the colossal statues of Memnon and Danaus at Thebes.

Ramses I. founded the nineteenth dynasty about B.C. 1462. His son, Seti I., built the great hall of columns at Karnak and the chief temple of Abydos, *Seti I.* overran Palestine, overcame the Hittites, and conquered the Libyans, who invaded Egypt from the west. His son, Ramses II. (Sesostris of the Greeks), was the greatest monarch of Egypt, and reigned for about seventy years. All the neighbouring powers in turn were attacked by him with varying results, on the whole favourable to Egypt. The Israelites built for *Ramses II.* this king the treasure cities of Pithom and Ramses. Huge statues of him were set up in several places, and his great buildings were exceedingly numerous. Even in Nubia, at Abu-Simbel, he set up a huge temple, its entrance being guarded by four colossal figures. It is impossible to say with certainty when *Exodus of the Israelites.* the Exodus of the Israelites from Egypt took place, but their oppression under Ramses II. is certain; and the weight of evidence favours the belief that the Exodus occurred towards the close of the nineteenth dynasty, and perhaps under Meneptah II., the son and successor of Ramses II. Ramses III. ruled over Egypt after nearly all its foreign possessions had' been lost; and he had to meet attacks from Phœnicians, Greeks, Libyans, and negroes. He revived the fading glories of Egypt, taking much spoil from his enemies, and restoring the maritime and mining interests of the country. New temples and palaces also were built.

But Egypt had commenced to decline. The kings of the twenty-second dynasty, however, endeavoured to regain power in Palestine, and settled many Semites, *Decline of* negroes, and other foreigners in Egypt; but *Egypt.* after a time Assyria defeated Egypt, which relapsed into a number of petty principalities. The twenty-sixth dynasty again revived Egyptian power. Psammetichus was able to restore temples and build fresh monuments. His son, Necho II., endeavoured to make a canal between the Red Sea and the Nile. Under his direction Africa appears to have been circumnavigated by Phœnician mariners in the sixth century B.C. He *Conquest by* fought against Josiah, king of Judah, and slew *the Persians.* him; but his onward progress was stopped by Nebuchadnezzar, who afterwards conquered Egypt, though not permanently. Cambyses, son of Cyrus of Persia, conquered Egypt about B.C. 525, and adopted the style of an Egyptian monarch, but later vented his anger at certain reverses upon Egyptian monuments and temples. After an inglorious revival, about B.C. 340 took place the final fall of the Egyptian monarchy, and since then no *Later* native prince has ruled in Egypt. Alexander, *conquerors.* the Greek Ptolemies, Rome, the Arab Mahometans, the Saracens, the Mamelukes, and the Turks in succession have dominated Egypt and made the natives their pawns. Never, till the English, in 1882, established themselves as guardians of order in Egypt, were the people considered or their interests protected. The recent short-lived annexation of the Soudan has failed; but Egypt was not strong in itself, and had no strength to spare for holding an unwilling population of Arabs and negroes in subjection.

The Egyptians of the great time of the Empire and the monuments were of a different type from the older people. They had oval faces and were round-headed, not long-headed, with small foreheads, large black eyes, long straight noses, somewhat full lips, small chins, and black, crisp, coarse, long hair. The men had dark-brown complexions; the women were lighter, ranging from olive to rose-pink. The men wore kilts to the knees, with girdles, and some-times a long garment of fine linen over the kilt. Beards were worn short and full, an inch long in general, while the king wore his three inches long and peculiarly plaited. Sandals were sometimes worn, but men often went barefoot. The lower classes shaved both head and face. Women were not markedly distinguished by dress from men, the kilt or skirt being tighter, and in the lower classes being the only garment.

Physical characters of ancient Egyptians.

Dress.

The Egyptian religion was a mixture of monotheism, polytheism, and animal worship. Which of these arose first, it is impossible to say. Many of their deities exhibited animal heads upon human bodies. Each great city had its own gods, at the head of whom stood a sun-god, worshipped as Ptah at Memphis, Osiris at This and Abydos, Amen-ra at Thebes, Ra at Heliopolis, etc. Apis, the bull, is a type of the animal gods. The complex mythologies which have been made out cannot be entered into here. But in later times a rationalist interpretation arose, which regarded all the divinities and spirits as varied manifestations of one divine essence. As in almost all other religions, the priesthood early became more important than the religion, and gained a leading place in the State. The priests, setting up the ideal that those who were justified before Osiris by their conduct on earth gained eternal happiness, assigned this blessing to every one who could pay for a sculptured record, for incantations and charms, and elaborate embalming. As to the future state, in the early empire, judging by the tomb of Ti at Sakkarah, the dead were believed to live over again their earthly life.

Egyptian religion.

The priesthood.

Egyptian architecture probably ranks next to Greek in the ancient world. Massiveness and durability were

(From a Photograph of the Mummy.)

8

RAMSES II., CALLED "THE GREAT," THE PHARAOH OF THE HEBREW OPPRESSION.
(From a Photograph of the Mummy.)

9

its first characteristics; next came faithfulness to nature
and idealising power. Their colour is never
Egyptian architecture. a prominent feature, and perspective was not
studied. The splendid temples of the Middle Empire
appear to have been intended for processions, and their
inner walls are covered with fine bas-reliefs and paintings.

It is a marked tribute to ideas of future existence, that
in Egypt every man, the king above all, sought to make
Embalming and burial. a fine tomb for himself; and the funeral rites
were the most elaborate. Embalming the body
and forming a mummy to last for ages occupied a long
time. Enfolded in covering after covering, the mummy
was at last placed in a stone sarcophagus, and then in a
sepulchral chamber, forming part of a family mausoleum.
Customary burial offerings were made several times a
year by the deceased's family.

Much has been learnt about Egyptian funeral ceremonies
from their chief religious book, the Book of the Dead,
The Book of the Dead. describing "the adventures of the soul after
death, and the texts it must quote in order to
escape the torments and trials of the lower world."
Egyptian literature is on the whole poor, the historical
Language. records being inflated panegyrics. The Egyptian language, which in its later form is called
Coptic, is Semitic in grammar, and in many of its roots;
but it is strikingly monosyllabic, and may have some
African elements in it. In Coptic, the language of the
Christianised Egyptians, many Greek words are introduced, and it is written with Greek characters and six
added letters from the later Egyptian.

The Egyptian hieroglyphics, or pictorial writings, were
already in full development in the age of Menes. Each
Hiero- glyphics. character also stood for one or more syllables,
and several of them represent single letters.
From the hieroglyphics the running-hand, or hieratic
writing, was developed.

The industrial arts were highly developed by the
Egyptians. In particular their linen weaving was first-
rate. In glass making, pottery, metal work, domestic
utensils and furniture, they had great skill. Their science

was quite as remarkable. Astronomy and geometry made considerable progress, and the mechanical **Arts and** skill they showed in the cutting and removal **sciences.** of huge stones is almost inexplicable. In the Middle Empire medicine had made great advances, many diseases being minutely described, and treatment by draughts, blisters, powders, etc., being adopted. Later, conservatism came in, and a doctor recommending new treatment did so at the risk of his life if the patient died. Many musical instruments were in use, and music and dancing were much employed in processions and in entertainments.

THE MODERN EGYPTIANS.

"Egypt is the Nile," it has been well said; and its ancient name, Kem (the black land), refers to the black colour of the soil, which has been produced by **Importance** the Nile inundations. Receiving the bulk of **of the Nile.** the harvest brought down from Equatorial Africa to the north, and surrounded on either side by deserts and mountains, Egypt has gained an importance quite out of proportion to its cultivable land. Scarcely six thousand square miles are actually under cultivation north of the first cataract, and their produce was the basis on which commerce, arts and sciences, and wide-reaching dominion arose. In the great era of Egypt, it must have been much more thickly peopled than now; and it continued largely peopled in spite of oppression and destructive wars. We must attribute its present inferiority of population especially to the Turks, a people with a genius for extracting almost everything of value from the peoples they rule. Fortunately they have every day less and less power to wrong the Egyptians.

Independently of foreigners—Turks, Syrians, Greeks, Armenians, Jews, Italians, French, and English—Egypt includes people of two sharply distinct religions **The fellahs.** —the Mahometans and the Coptic Christians. The Mahometans constitute seven-eighths of the population; and it is astonishing how considerably they resemble the ancient Egyptians, in spite of the repeated introduction of Arabs and Semites of other types. And, following the best opinion, we must regard the mass of the Egyptians as representing the ancient people, with a dash of negro and a considerable mixture of Arab blood. The true Egyptians are the fellaheen, or peasants. They are of medium height, inclining to tallness, robust and well-made, slim and lithe, capable of great endurance. They have oval faces, broad brows, brown complexions, and brilliant black eyes, often kept half-closed in the brilliant sunlight; a well-formed mouth, with rather full lips and beautiful teeth; and a straight nose with rather wide nostrils. The head is usually shaved, except a tuft on the top. The moustache and beard, though unshaven, do not grow long.

Egyptian women mature early, and many girls are mothers at fourteen; but they have a correspondingly early decline into ugliness. The complexions of the women are not so dark as those of the men, owing to their less exposure to the sun and the extent to which they go veiled. "The eyes," says Mr. Lane ("Modern Egyptians"), "with very few exceptions are black, large, and of a long almond form, with long, beautiful lashes, and an exquisitely soft bewitching expression—eyes more beautiful can hardly be conceived." "Few lovelier women," says Mr. Stanley Lane-Poole, "can be seen than the Egyptian peasant-girl of sixteen returning from her usual errand of fetching water from the river or the village well; her lithe form suffers no ungainly strain from the weight of the great water-jar she carries on her head,—balanced so securely that it scarcely needs the steadying of the shapely brown arm,—and she walks erect with a noble carriage." But the picture is partly spoiled by heavy blue tattooing and dyeing on chin, hands, and arms, and between the breasts; and great rings in ears and nose, bangles, and other ornaments testify to the female love for personal adornment, further manifested by the blackening of the eyelids with kohl and other cosmetics.

The usual peasants' dress is a sort of smock or shirt of cotton or wool, some only wearing drawers underneath.

The head-covering is a red fez, round which those who can afford it wind a turban. The peasant **Peasants' dress.** women wear a still shorter gown of similar material, with cotton drawers or trousers, and a head-veil.

The food of the peasantry consists of millet or maize bread, milk and cheese, small salt fish, cucumbers and gourds, onions, lentils, beans and other pulse, **Food.** and dates. They seldom taste flesh meat. The women are in great subjection, often not eating with their husbands, carrying all burdens, and doing all drudgery. In a number of respects the peasantry are in a low state of morals and intelligence, though patient and **Character.** enduring almost beyond belief. Many of the worst Bedouin customs cling to them. Family and tribal feuds persist, and blood revenge is exacted. Unfaithfulness in a wife is often punished with death. But, as Mr. Stanley Lane-Poole says, many of his vices are the vices of servitude. "He has been so long trampled down, that he has forgotten how to stand upright; he has been so systematically robbed, that he tries a little thieving on his own account; he is the victim of such rapacious greed, that he has become avaricious himself; he has known so much of the lies of his rulers, that he has found it useful to lie to them in return." Fortunately, under English influence, the exactions to which the fellah had formerly to submit have been much reduced and made more gentle in their mode of levying; and forced labour on public works is largely discontinued and on the way to complete abandonment.

The Copts, or Christian descendants of the ancient Egyptians, are not more than 150,000. Although in early Christian times they mixed much with Greeks **The Copts.** and Abyssinians, they are wonderfully like the Egyptians of the monuments, and differ so little in features from the fellaheen that it is not necessary to describe them separately. They have their own patriarch, bishops, priests, monks, etc., and a separate liturgy in the ancient Coptic tongue, now not used in conversation. In many respects the Copts have practices like those of the ancient Jews, but in others they have imitated the Mahometans.

They are strictly forbidden to marry out of their sect, and this rule is almost always observed. They are very bigoted in their religious views, being as hostile to other Christians as Mahometans. Sullenness, too, is an unfavourable trait; and a respectable Copt told Mr. Lane that his people were generally deceitful, and abandoned to the pursuit of gain and to sensual pleasures, and that the priests were not better than the people. That they have intelligence is evident from the fact that they are very generally employed as scribes and accountants in Egypt; comparatively few are tradesmen.

The upper classes of Egypt are becoming continually more Europeanised. The numerous European officials, The upper even the modern Turks, act as a strong Euro-classes. peanising element, and the influence of the numerous European tourists and residents tends in the same direction. One might say that the red fez, always worn, and the gauze veils concealing the harem ladies in the boxes of the opera, were the principal public signs of a former state of things as to the well-to-do people. But the middle and lower classes amply retain their customs and their Oriental appearance. The trading quarters are crowded with small shops, and are very irregular, as are most of the streets, except the modern European ones.

Habits. The tradesmen occupy themselves in sitting, smoking, waiting for customers, or bargaining with them in a formal and slow, though sufficiently exciting style, everything being conducted with great politeness. Early rising, early ablutions, prayer at sunrise, are among the virtues of the majority; but sloth in other things is an article of practice if not of creed. Coffee and tobacco are the ever-present comforts. Food is not much longed for or greatly indulged in in the daytime, the townsfolk's fare being not very greatly superior to that of the fellah. Supper is the great meal, at which much bread or unleavened cake, with beans, fish, or meat, lentils, etc., all brought on the tray or table together, are eaten promiscuously.

The men of the middle and upper classes (when not Europeanised) wear full drawers of linen or cotton, a shirt

with full sleeves, a short vest over it in winter, and over
this a long vest of striped silk and cotton, **Dress of**
called the kaftan, reaching to the ankles. The **men.**
sleeves also are capable of completely covering the hands.
Round the kaftan a piece of white muslin or a coloured
shawl is wound as a girdle. In addition, for full dress,
a great cloth robe or coat is worn. The small cotton
cap, red fez, and turban form the head-dress. Thick red
morocco shoes cover the feet, without stockings. One of
the most essential accompaniments of dress is a silver

signet-ring, with a
stone engraved with
the wearer's name
and some word sig-
nifying worshipper
or servant of God.
This is used for
sealing documents,
signing letters, etc.
The lower classes in
the towns wear a
simplified set of gar-
ments of coarser
materials.

The Egyptian
women of the middle
and upper classes
dress richly and ele-
gantly. The under-
skirt is shorter and

FELLAHEEN.

fuller than the men's, while the trousers are fuller and
longer. The long vest, much like the kaf- **Dress of**
tan of the men, is tighter, and has longer **women.**
sleeves; it buttons down the front, but leaves a considerable part of the bosom uncovered. A shawl or kerchief
forms a loose girdle. Over this is a long embroidered
robe of cloth, velvet, or silk, or a shorter jacket. The
turban is worn in a high, flat shape, very different from
that of the men. Many wear house shoes or slippers of
yellow or red morocco. This is the indoor costume; but

for out-of-doors use a large, loose gown with extremely wide sleeves is donned, a long face-veil of white muslin, concealing the face below the eyes, and reaching to the feet.   Over all is the great silk habarah.   Lower-class women wear various degrees of less elaborate clothing, and many of them never conceal their faces.

It is remarkable in how slovenly a way the children are dressed, even among the wealthy, who treat them **Children.** very indulgently in every way.   With this a strict obedience and dutifulness to parents are

FELLAHEEN.

inculcated.   Circumcision is general, the ceremony taking place at the age of five or six, with much parade.   Parents do not give their children much training themselves, the elementary teaching of the Mahometan religion constituting the bulk of it.   The native schoolmaster teaches them reading and to recite parts of the Koran; but lately many improved schools have been established in the towns, and education is beginning to have a chance.

Houses in Cairo vary from one to three storeys in height, with flat roofs, and windows and balconies latticed round.

The lowest floor is partly raised above the ground. The doors have usually a text from the Koran **Houses.** upon them, supposed to protect from the evil eye. They are fastened with a wooden bolt, and an iron ring serves as a knocker. The houses have inner courts with rooms all round.

The great hindrance to true moral progress in Egypt is not polygamy, which is infrequent, but divorce, which is very prevalent for slight causes. Slavery is **Divorce and** not yet abolished; and until it is, there will be **slavery.** much moral evil arising out of it. Yet slaves are not,

EGYPTIAN MUSICAL INSTRUMENTS, PIPE, ORNAMENTS, ETC.

as a rule, ill-treated, and frequently rise high in their master's or mistress's favour.

Mr. Lane gave as the most remarkable characteristic of the modern Egyptians, their religious pride, leading to much hypocrisy and religious ostentation. The **Religious** hundreds of mosques in Cairo may be taken as **pride.** a proof of this, or of true religious zeal. The unoccupied Mussulman will often utter pious ejaculations. The shop-keeper often recites chapters in the Koran, or his prayers and praises, in the hearing of the passers-by. On the most ordinary occasions he prefaces an act by the words, "In the name of God, the Compassionate, the Merciful;"

and after it is over, "Praise be to God."   The most sinful things will be done or related, and the offence is condoned by saying, "I beg forgiveness of God."   The most extravagant honour is paid to Mahomet and the Koran; and printed books are much objected to, because the ink and paper, which will print the name of Allah, so often occurring in all their books, will almost certainly be impure.

Belief in predestination and fatalism are almost equally characteristic of the Egyptian Mahometan. "The me **Fatalism.** display, in times of distressing uncertainty, an exemplary patience, and after any afflicting event, a remarkable degree of resignation and fortitude"; but the women, in circumstances of grief, give way to extravagant cries and shrieks.

Formerly the Egyptians had a good character for their treatment of domestic animals; but now they have degenerated much. Both dogs and donkeys are savagely maltreated.

The Egyptians are hospitable and cheerful towards each other as well as to strangers. Intoxication is ex- **Habits and character.** tremely rare. Cleanliness is very general, in spite of the fact that all water comes from the Nile and that the services of a multitude of water-carriers are necessary to provide for the required ablutions.   Their love of country and of home is notable, and one might say this was a form of their indolence. Their obstinacy and conservatism are great. It must be allowed too that for sensualism a great proportion of the town Egyptians cannot easily be surpassed.

But Egypt, like India or China, requires at least a volume to do it justice. Space fails us to deal with the **Miscellaneous peoples.** festivals, the ceremonies, the amusements, and the various features of interest in the land of the Pharaohs. Nor must we recount here the characteristics of the Bedouin Arabs, who are to be found in large numbers outside the settled tracts of Egypt—who breed cattle, sheep, and camels, conduct caravans, make charcoal and matting. Their numerous tribes are not infrequently at war with one another. Turks are comparatively few in Egypt, but exercise a good deal of influence. Levantines (of Greek, Syrian, and Italian stock) are much more numerous, and carry on very profitable trades. The European element is at least 100,000 strong in Egypt, and is likely to increase. Black slaves and servants do not decrease in number, though the public traffic in them is stopped. Gipsies are numerous, and are known by the name of Ghajars. They lay themselves out for the amusement of the populace, being dancers, jugglers, fortune-tellers, tattooers, serpent charmers, etc.

A few words must be devoted to the diseases of Egypt which show themselves so evidently. Diseases of the eyes, due to heat, dryness of air, and sand-storms, are painfully frequent; and they are aggravated by the great number of flies. There is no country in the world where blind people are so numerous. Anæmia, due to insufficient food, is very prevalent, as also is dysentery. But the almost entire cessation of plague and cholera, owing to improved sanitary arrangements, has tended greatly to increase the population; leprosy and elephantiasis are unfortunately by no means extinct.

CHAPTER II.
The Inhabitants of Northern Africa.

Mauretania—Mahometan conquests—The Spaniards and Portuguese—Moorish piracy—Battle of Tetuan—The Numidians—Turkish rule in Algiers—Algerian piracy—The Deys of Algiers—British expedition—French conquest—Native risings—Abd-el-Kader—Carthage—Conquests and greatness — Expulsion from Sicily — Hannibal—Destruction of Carthage—Second rise and fall—Tunis in the past—Tripoli and Cyrenaica—The Berbers—Physical characters—Mixed origin—Rock dwellings—Nomad tribes—Marriage—Clothing—The Berbers in Morocco—Food—Independent character—Government—The Kabyle of Algiers—Berber tribes of the Sahara—The Uled-Delim—The Guanches—The Tuareg—Physical characters — Veiling — Taste in colour—Moral character—Position of women—Religion—Negroes in Tripoli—Fezzan—The Tibbu—Physical characters—Morals and customs—Arabs of Northern Africa—Physical characters—Arabs of the towns—The City of Tunis—Kairwan—The North African Jews — Tunis Jews—Products and industries.

TUAREG.

UNDER this head we group the inhabitants of Morocco, Algiers, Tunis, Tripoli, and the Sahara, who have much in common. Something has been known of them for a long period, and both the native Numidians, Moors, and others, and the Phœnician colonists of Carthage and the Mussulman Arabs played a notable part in history. In modern times, however, they have occupied a comparatively unimportant position in politics.

Morocco, Algeria, and Tunis were very early inhabited by a race of dolmen, cromlech, and barrow builders, who buried their dead with the knees drawn up to the chin. At Imzorah, south-east of Azila, are some extraordinary megalithic monuments, one group consisting of a circle of sixty-seven great stones, the largest twenty feet high, placed round a mound. There is indisputable evidence also of the existence in Northern Africa of a more ancient people who used rough flint implements, and of a later people who used polished flint and stone implements. Later came a bronze age. Under the dolmens have been found skeletons and crania of two types, both long-headed, one taller, with its highest point behind the middle, the other with its apex just above the ears.

Morocco and part of Algeria were included in the old Roman province Mauretania, the land of the Mauri or Moors, probably the ancestors of the modern **Mauretania.** Berbers and Tuaregs. From the time of the Jugurthine war (110–106 B.C.), they were known to the Romans, who allowed them to remain independent till, in 42 A.D., they were formed into two provinces of the Empire, which retained them till the Vandals conquered them in 429. Although the Eastern empire of Byzantium recovered Mauretania by the generalship of Belisarius in 533, it was subdued by the Mussulman Arabs towards the end of the seventh century, after obstinate resistance on the part of the Berbers. Later, the country **Mahometan** was divided between numerous small States, **conquest.** till, early in the tenth century, the Fatimite caliphs, in alliance with the Berbers, gained possession of the country. About the middle of the eleventh century the dynasty of the Almoravides arose from the enthusiasm of an Arab named Abdallah, who combined under his leadership a large number of Berbers, and conquered a great part of North-west Africa and Spain. In the next century the dynasty of the Almohades, founded by Mohammed-Ibn-Abdallah, succeeded them in power. Since this time the history of Morocco has presented little but constant

turbulence, instability, and bloodshed, combined with
continued hostility to Europeans and to Christianity.   In the fifteenth and sixteenth centuries
the Portuguese and Spaniards, after having

The Spaniards and Portuguese.

finally driven the Moors from Europe, attacked them at
home, and took Ceuta, Tangiers, and other places.
In the seventeenth and eighteenth centuries tho
Moors regained much of these conquests, and by piracy,

Moorish piracy.

slavery, and extortion of ransom, inflicted constant annoyance on Europeans. It is worth recalling, that in 1662 the Portuguese handed over Tangiers to us as part of the dowry of Catherine of Braganza, queen of Charles II.; but we let it slip from us in 1684. By this time the ruler of Morocco had taken the title of Sultan, still retained by his successors. The traditional policy of Morocco has been kept up during the present century, for the Moors aided Abd-el-Kader against the French, and constantly resisted Spanish efforts to recover old rights and possessions and gain new ones. The battle of Tetuan **Battle of** (1860), however, in which General O'Donnell **Tetuan.** and the Spaniards were victors, secured increased Spanish influence over Morocco, and prepared the way for the admission of Europeans to trade all over the Empire.

The Massyli and Massæsyli are well known in Roman history as the early inhabitants of Algiers, the former of whom, under Massinissa, supported Rome against Hannibal; the latter, under Syphax, supporting Hannibal. **The** On the defeat of Hannibal, the two peoples **Numidians.** were placed under Massinissa, who was then termed the king of Numidia. This was however but the prelude to the formation of the province of Mauretania, as already described. For a long time the history of Algiers was similar to that of Morocco. The Spaniards took Algiers in 1509, and to expel them, the natives, in 1516, invited the aid of Barbarossa, a Greek who became a Mussulman and had made himself a name as a Turkish **Turkish rule** piratical leader. He speedily drove out the **in Algiers.** Spaniards and made himself master of the country. His brother, who succeeded him, placed himself under the protection of Turkey, and thenceforward his family reigned under the title of pasha or viceroy of Algiers. At the same time a terrible system of piracy was **Algerian** established in the Mediterranean; and by the **piracy.** labour of vast numbers of captives the port of Algiers was made both formidable and safe against the sea. In spite of continued efforts by the European powers, piracy continued, many expeditions being defeated or foiled by the Algerines. In 1710, the Turkish pasha was expelled, and the Dey, or leader of the Janissaries, who had long exercised great power, became supreme. Nothing effective was done to suppress Algerian piracy till 1816, when the British expedition under Lord Exmouth bombarded Algiers and secured the liberation of 1,200 Christian slaves, and a promise to suppress piracy. But the promise was soon forgotten, and Algiers rendered more formidable than ever. At last France resolved to take effective measures, and in 1830, Admiral Duperré and General Bourmont accomplished the conquest of Algiers, the Dey retiring to Naples, and the Turkish troops being expelled from the country.

Unfortunately the French, in consolidating their conquest, did not respect the religious prejudices of the people. They even destroyed some mosques, appropriated land set apart for religious purposes, and attempted to enforce European usages. Consequently for many years they were harassed by constant risings of Arabs and Kabyles, and the French measures of retaliation were frequently very cruel. About 1832, the celebrated Arab chief Abd-el-Kader took the field against the French; and although for a short time in nominal subjection to them, he maintained throughout many years of warfare an unconquerable spirit of independence, and many times defeated the invaders. Although he was at last captured, in 1847, yet in subsequent years Arabs and Kabyles frequently rose against the French, and vast numbers perished on both sides. It was not till 1871 that the colony was emancipated from military rule and treated as an ordinary portion of French territory, since which a great improvement has taken place. Many colonists from Alsace-Lorraine have settled here, and the European population has largely increased.

The next portion of Northern Africa, to the east of Algiers, is now called after the city of Tunis, but was formerly much more famous under the rule of Carthage, the rival of Rome, which was founded in the Bay of Tunis, in the middle of the ninth century B.C., by Phœnician colonists, who had already several flourishing settlements along that coast, including Utica, Tunis, and Hippo. Carthage gradually acquired predominance over her neighbours, became commercially important, and acquired territory from the Straits of Gibraltar to the Great Syrtis (Gulf of Sidra), in addition

A MOORISH STROLLING MINSTREL.

to Sardinia, the Balearic Islands, and Malta. Although the Carthaginians subdued the natives of Africa in contact with them, they failed to assimilate them, and to this their final downfall may be attributed as much as to the superior power and genius

Conquests and greatness.

of the Romans. At one period, in the fifth century B.C., Carthage was unmistakably stronger than Rome, and could dictate limits to her rival within which trading might be carried on. About 500 B.C., Carthaginian enterprise extended so far as to found colonies (under Hanno) on the West Coast of Africa, probably down to the Gambia, and to discover Britain (under Himilco). The protracted endeavours of Carthage to subdue Sicily first led to attacks by the Romans, who, in the First Punic War, drove them from that island (242 B.C.). The Carthaginians, foiled in Sicily, turned their attention to Spain; and the great Hannibal attempted to make Spain the stepping-stone for conquering Rome. Every one knows the unsurpassed skill and courage with which he long maintained the struggle, and the disastrous end of his ambition. The battle of Zama, in B.C. 202, put an end to Carthage as a military power; but it was reserved for Cato to reiterate the terrible words, "Delenda est Carthago," and to carry them out ruthlessly. In 146 B.C., Carthage was burnt, and its site ploughed over.

Expulsion from Sicily.

Hannibal.

Destruction of Carthage.

Carthage was colonised by Rome in B.C. 29, and again became notable, almost rivalling Alexandria. The Vandals made it the capital of their African kingdom in the fifth century; but in 706 it was utterly destroyed by the Mahometans.

Second rise and fall.

Thus perished a city which must rank only after Athens and Rome. Unfortunately the Romans were too bitterly hostile to do it justice, and too destructive of a hated rival to leave many remains by which we could adequately judge Carthage. We know little beyond the facts that Carthage had an aristocratic government, in which the people, however, had some share; and that they inherited from the Phœnicians a spirit of religious devotion. The disinterring of monuments, coins, and inscriptions may do much in the future to enlighten us about Carthage.

Tunis early became Christianised, and gave birth to the fathers Tertullian, Cyprian, and Augustine; but was overrun by the Arabs in the seventh century A.D., and Christianity became completely extinct

Tunis in the past.

there. After a time Tunis became an independent Mahometan State, until, in 1575, it was forced to accept the control of the Turks. This however was not rigorously exercised, and the Bey became practically independent, but received investiture from the Sultan of Turkey. In 1881, the French invaded the country, on the pretext of chastising a border tribe, the Kroumirs, for raids on Algeria; and they ended by establishing themselves in Tunis, and taking over the management of affairs.

Tripoli and Barca, occupying the coast territory between Tunis and Egypt, represent the ancient Cyrenaica or Pentapolis. The chief city, **Tripoli and Cyrenaica.** Cyrene, was founded, in 631 B.C., by a Greek colony from the island of Thera, and soon other cities arose; and the name Pentapolis was given to the country from its having five principal cities, Berenice, Barce, Cyrene, Apollonia, and Arsinoë. The Ptolemies exercised control over the country;

MOORISH WOMAN, TANGIERS.

the last of them bequeathed it to the Romans, and it became a Roman province, and prospered greatly in commerce. Jews settled in it largely, and in Trajan's time raised a formidable revolt against Rome. On its suppression, after much slaughter, the prosperity of the country diminished, and the uncivilised native tribes regained much of their land. In the seventh century, the Mahometan Arabs overran it; and although the Christians, under Roger II. of Sicily, regained it for a short time in the twelfth century, the Arabs again conquered it and held it till 1510, when the Spaniards took it from them. The Emperor Charles V. gave it, together with Malta, in 1530, to the Knights of St. John; but, in 1551 it was conquered by the Turks, who have retained it in more or less nominal subjection ever since. The districts of the Sahara, which are naturally connected with Northern Africa, have no history properly so called.

The Berbers, a branch of the Hamites, and probably related to the ancient Egyptians, are the main and original inhabitants of Northern Africa, representing those whom the Romans called Numidians, and whose nomad habits they described. From the name Berber was derived the term Barbary, formerly given to North-west Africa. In many parts they are much mixed with Arabs, who came as Mahometan invaders. At least two-thirds of the inhabitants are Berbers, though in the North they are usually called Kabyles. Probably it may in the future be proved that the Iberians extended into Northern Africa, and contributed to form the Berber type. These people are divided into a great many tribes, continually at war with one another, and further distracted by family feuds. In many parts they can be clearly distinguished from Arabs by their wider and fuller faces, less regular features, more arched eyebrows, more sparkling eyes, and somewhat lighter hair. The nose is rarely aquiline and is often large and short, the chin prominent, the mouth rather large and thick-lipped. They have also much more gaiety, dash, and enterprise, and are more frank.

BERBER WOMAN.

The Berbers.

Physical characters.

After careful study, it appears that the Berbers them
selves are much mixed, including people of very different
height, conformation of limbs, form of skull, **Mixed origin.**
and colour of hair and skin.   Even fair and
red-skinned people may be found in the North, while the
majority are of a brown complexion and colour. Some
have even blue eyes. Evident descendants of the Romans

may be found at
Tebesra in Al-
giers, calling
themselves so,
although being
Mahometans by
religion. On the
whole, we may
describe the popu-
lation of Northern
Africa as derived
from Italian,
Spanish, Asiatic,
Egyptian, and
negro invasions
and intermix-
tures. But all
speak one or both
of two types of
language, the
Berber and the
Arabic. The
Berber group of
languages is re-
lated to the
Semitic, not in

ARAB GIRL, ALGIERS.

vocabulary, but in grammar and in its guttural sounds.
It has been classified with the Coptic and Abyssinian
languages as Hamitic.

There is a most evident contrast between the Berber
populations, according as they are settled in   **Rock**
towns or live a nomad life. In some parts the   **dwellings.**
wild tribes still live in rock-dwellings, hollowed out arti-

ficially so as to form houses of more than one storey. At Zenthan in Tripoli there are from a thousand to twelve hundred of these dwellings, inhabited by about 6000 people, whose chief support is derived from the cultivation of olives, and who during harvest-time live in tents.

Nomad tribes. Not unfrequently the main support of the nomad tribes has been derived from war and plunder, and in these pursuits they showed very few scruples. Nowadays they find plunder less possible; and in the French territories many of them are settling in the towns, and occupying themselves as porters.

The Berbers have not adopted from their Mahometan conquerors the practice of polygamy, and women hold a **Marriage.** higher place among them than among Arabs. Their women in most parts go freely unveiled, and the sexes have free conversation with one another. Marriages are arranged by parents or relatives, and a price is paid by the husband's side, returnable if a divorce follows without the wife being in fault. Divorce is however frequent, being little interfered with by Mahometan ideas. In some tribes the women have preserved the ancient habit of tattooing themselves; and some of these tattoo themselves with a cross, a relic of early Christianity.

Clothing is very simple, yet varies from tribe to tribe. Frequently the sole garment of both sexes is a sort of **Clothing.** woollen or cotton tunic, fastened round the shoulders. Children are, in Morocco, habitually carried hooked round their mother's hips in a fold of the tunic, and hence a majority of the people have legs bent outwards.

A large number of the Berbers of Morocco live in stone houses, sometimes grouped into defensible villages, and **Berbers in Morocco.** even in some cases forming true strongholds. But many are nomads living wholly in tents, and others live a great part of the year in tents, which are of a beehive shape. In some cases these are covered with black stuff made of camels' hair or palm-fibre. The support consists of two upright poles, connected by a cross-piece, and the whole is not more than eight feet high. A partition may divide these tents into two rooms·

but the furniture is very simple, including however apparatus for grinding corn, a spinning-wheel, and a mirror. There are tents or houses set apart for strangers, and hospitality is carefully observed.

Cakes and fruits are the chief food, flesh being a rare

TUAREG.

luxury. Water is the principal drink, spirits being little known except in the towns. But where grapes flourish, wine abounds and is freely drunk during vin- **Food.** tage-time. Men eat separately from women and children; and the fingers are the chief implements of eating. Tobacco and hashish (the dried tops of hemp) are largely smoked.

On the whole, the Berbers have largely preserved their independence of conquerors, as well as their want of cohe-sion. They are not faithful to their promises, nor easily induced to do anything that does not accord with their primitive ideas of freedom. Taxation they will only submit to on compulsion, often attempting to evade all law by removing or evacuating their settlements. Often they will treat with rulers only on condition of the recognition of their equality with them. In fact, their air of independence is communicated even to their women, not a few of whom bear arms.

Independent character.

The tribes are governed mainly in a patriarchal manner, the head of the family or of the tribe being supreme. Assemblies of the family or of the tribe are held, and their views are considerably regarded. Confederations and alliances of tribes do however exist, but they are on the whole loose and easily broken up. Some tribes elect a chief for a year, but it is rarely that he can command implicit obedience. The Berbers have long ceased to produce leaders of commanding ability, if they ever did so. Their chief part in history has been accomplished under Arab leadership.

Government.

The Kabyles of Algiers appear to be the most settled of the Berbers. They live on the higher lands of the eastern Atlas, and grow corn, fruits, and pota-toes, cultivating their land carefully and industriously, as well as learning to work in lead, iron, and copper. They are very socially inclined, and are described as having a truly democratic government in their villages and communities. They dislike and keep aloof from the Arabs,—by no means a bad sign,—and do not show anything like their religious fanaticism. They are largely governed by a set of customs or canons handed down by tradition, many of which undoubtedly have a Christian origin. The prayers, prostrations, and fastings of Mahometanism are little adopted by them. They even eat of the wild boar, forbidden by the Koran. Scarcely a hundred Kabyles a year make the pilgrimage to Mecca, and these

The Kabyles of Algiers.

chiefly go as merchants. Their ceremonies, such as they observe, have a manifest relation to nature-worship.

The inhabitable oases and borders of the Sahara are chiefly inhabited by people of Berber tribes, who, as herdsmen, find a good subsistence where water **Berber tribes** is at all plentiful. In the south-west their **of the** skins, always uncovered from the waist up- **Sahara.** wards, are reddish-coloured; the women are unveiled, but wear a long flowing robe. They are very peacefully disposed, and bear the reputation of being Marabouts, or Mahometan devotees. Women have a high position among them, being much less hardworked than among many other Mahometan people. Unfortunately, both sexes have an almost invincible dislike to washing.

NOMAD WOMAN OF TUNIS.

One of the interesting groups of tribes of the Western Sahara, occupying the territory of Tiris, is called Uled-Delim, partly traders with caravans, partly **The** plunderers. Their women have much beauty, **Uled-Delim.** with delicate feet and hands, and finger-nails stained with henna. They have remarkably large eyes, long eyelashes, and noses which remind the beholder of Greek women, combined with a slender figure. Some of the Berbers have village settlements, and are agricultural—growing dates, millet, maize, and other grains; others are sea fishermen, and their nets appear to gain a very rich harvest.

A word may here be given to the original inhabitants of the Canary Islands, known as Guanches, who were un-doubtedly related to the Berbers; but they had **The Guanches.** probably settled there before the Berbers had heard of Christianity or Mahometanism; for when the Spaniards, in the fourteenth century, subdued them, they had no metals, and ploughed with bullocks' horns. They believed both in a Supreme Being and in a malignant spirit, and also in a future state. An interesting feature, indicating their relationship to the ancient Egyptians, was, that they embalmed their dead—placing the mummies erect in caverns in the mountain sides; the mummies of chiefs had a staff placed in their hands, and a vessel of milk at their sides. The Guanches were finally all exterminated or sold into slavery by the Spaniards. The islands are now inhabited by Spaniards, many of whom are mixed with descendants of the old inhabitants: the population is more than a quarter of a million.

The central regions of the Sahara are occupied by tribes known as Tuareg, or Tuarik, reaching northward to **The Tuareg.** the borders of Algeria and Tunis, and in the south touching the central Soudan — a land 1,200 miles from north to south, and likely long to afford a home to independent tribes. In these regions again and again expeditions have perished, or have returned baffled from them. The Arabs gave the inhabitants of this vast area the name Tuareg, "abandoned by God," because they so long resisted conversion to Mahometanism. They call themselves Imoshagh, as the Berbers of Morocco call themselves Imazigh—a word signifying their proud independence. They have some Arab mixture, but retain a type very much akin to the ancient Egyptian.

The Tuareg are mostly tall and thin, but powerful, of a bronzed complexion. Their long stride, although grave and slow, has a peculiar jerk. Some few have blue eyes, but most are dark-eyed. They are extremely **Physical** sober, and feed once a day upon dates and **characters.** other fruits, seeds, and a little meat. They suffer much from rheuma-tism and oph-thalmia, al-though their thick eyebrows and long eye-lashes greatly protect the eyes; and the men habitually veil the face to pro-tect themselves from **Veiling.** the glare of the sun's rays and their reflection from the sand. Even at night the men wear the veil, which, in the case of the richer, is black, while the poorer, often with negro blood in them, wear white veils. Strange to say, the women do not habitually veil themselves.

ARAB WCMAN OF TUNIS.

In the north, the men shave their heads, but retain a sort of crest, from the forehead to the back of the neck, which holds on the veil. Guns, lances, and swords are inseparable companions of these people. They use powdered indigo to make hands, arms, and faces blue,

and the rest of the body is covered with a blouse and
Taste in colour. pantaloons of the same colour; leather sandals, of course, are essential. The fashionable
colour for women, on the other hand, is yellow, obtained
from yellow ochre. Ablutions, though formally fulfilled
by a little rubbing with sand, are never really performed.

Opposite opinions have been expressed about the Tuareg
by different explorers; but it is undoubted that they have
Moral character. often been cruel, treacherous, and greedy, while
some have shown a noble fidelity and true
hospitality to Mussulmans. Some are much more savage
and cruel than others, the worst being those who get all
their work done by negro slaves.

The northern Tuareg maintain the rights of the eldest
son of the eldest sister to inherit property gained by force,
Position of women. while other property is shared equally by the
children. At the same time the blood of the
child is reckoned to be that of the mother: the son of a
male slave and of a woman of noble birth is noble; the
son of a noble father and a female slave is a slave. In
general, the women are regarded as at least the equals
of men; they give themselves in marriage, not before the
age of twenty, the parents having only a certain veto;
they keep their fortunes untouched, and are often richer
than their husbands; they bring up the children, and take
the lead at feasts, having the choice of what is best,
excepting coffee and tea, which are reserved for the men.
They may even, in some cases, take part in tribal affairs,
and attain the rank of female sheikh. Polygamy is
almost unknown, and divorce strictly limited. These
predominant women are described by M. Duveyrier as
genuine musicians, playing on and singing to several
instruments, and improvising songs; and even as knowing
how to read and write. The men are well up in the
movements of the stars and in local topography, but this
is the extent of their knowledge.

As to religion, the Tuareg show little zeal; they leave
Religion. the Marabouts to pray for them. But they
have some ceremonies and signs dating earlier
than Mahometanism; the cross is a sacred symbol, and

they call the genii of heaven "angelus." They do not weep for the dead, for fear of raising them to life again; and after a burial, they change their camp. The Marabouts, however few and little fanatical, are slowly leavening the people with Mahometanism. They decide points of conduct or law by the Koran; and the Tuareg very generally wear amulets and charms on neck, arms, legs, etc., containing verses from the Koran.

Coming to the Eastern Sahara, we meet with more and more of the true negro type. In Tripoli negroes are very numerous, largely owing to the extensive slave-trade still kept up from Central Africa across the desert, so terrible in its results that, as one traveller, Rohlfs, expressively says, "Any one who did not know the way to Bornu would only have to follow the bones of dead slaves, which lie right and left of the track." The Arab and Berber population of Tripoli is largely infused with negro blood. The negroes of Tripoli live to a great extent in separate villages of huts, made of palms and reeds; and many of the languages of Central Africa may be heard in these villages, although the Houssa prevails.   *Negroes in Tripoli.*

Passing south by various oases into Fezzan, we find a very barren country, but with garden-like oases covered with date-trees. Date-palms supply the food and shelter both of man and beast. Camels' milk, with a certain amount of grain, supplies almost the only other food. The inhabitants are a mixture of all peoples of past and present Northern Africa. Ethiopians, Berbers, Arabs, Italian captives, negroes of various regions, have all mingled here; and almost every shade, from fair to black, may be found. Some of the mixed negroes have long, straight hair, while some of the fair people have short, woolly hair. Murzuk, the capital, in a large oasis, is situated on a marshy and malarial site; and in summer has a deadly, pestilential atmosphere. Its site, however, was dictated by its convenience for the slave-trade.   *Fezzan.*

Passing over Ghadames, we come to the land of the negro Tibbu,—the "people of the rocks,"—a great number of them being true troglodytes, living either in natural caverns, or in spaces between great   *The Tibbu.*

rocks, roofed in by palm or acacia branches. The land
of the Tibbu is very extensive, occupying nearly all the
south-east Sahara district. For ten months in the year
drought prevails; only after the summer rains do the
camels get grass enough to give abundance of milk.
Dates, and the fruits of the doum palm, and cereals are
also eaten by them; but during the dry months they are
often reduced to eat the bitter-apple. Meat is very seldom in their *menu*, and then comes from the aged or
diseased animals; but it is valued in proportion to the
rarity of the dainty. It is carefully dried and pounded,
so that the bones are mingled with it, and the skin is
eaten.

Notwithstanding the scantiness of their diet, which
makes them very thin, the people are strong and very
active. They seldom rise beyond the middle
height, but are exceedingly well-proportioned.
In complexion they are among the lightest of the negro
type, and their nostrils are less flattened and their lips
less thick. They have longer and less frizzly hair than
the negroes of the Soudan, and their beard is somewhat
more abundant. Their women are by no means unattrac-
tive in youth, being both pleasing in expression and
strong. Both sexes are able to resist extreme hunger for
several days; and their enforced abstemiousness makes
them very free from disease.

Although the Tibbu of Tibesti have a bad reputation
for cruelty and treachery, Dr. Nachtigal was able to return in safety from his perilous journey among
them, described in his " Sahara and Soudan."
He found them extremely clever and cunning, greedy and
suspicious, supreme at a bargain, cruel, and hard-looking.
Laughter is but little heard among them, and wordy
wars are more to their liking than music and dancing.
Many of them wear knife scars on their temples as a
matter of fashion. Like the Tuareg, they have the custom
of veiling themselves. They have also several Arab customs, and have become strong Mahometans; but their
language is an original negro one, allied to those of
Bornu. Nachtigal says that, wide as is the tract of

country overspread by the Tibbu, they do not number in all more than 28,000. Chiefs, more or less powerful, rule over them; but custom is very powerful, and the chiefs have no army nor taxation. Birth is greatly vaunted, and women are valued — their usefulness and fidelity being highly spoken of. In Kawar, west of Tibesti, a so-called sultan rules over a small number of subjects.

The Arabs of Northern Africa are by no means favourably spoken of. They exhibit in intensity the vices of their race,—greed, treachery, and cruelty,—and **Arabs of Northern Africa.** are undoubtedly degenerate specimens of the race that spread Mahometanism over so large a portion of the globe. In some parts, especially in Morocco, they are much crossed with negroes, and have become almost black. This is the case even with the family of the Sultans of Morocco. This is. rather an improvement to them than otherwise, for the face becomes wider, not so long and narrow, the aquiline nose is softened, and the expression is gentler. But the religious fanaticism of the Arabs, when mixed with negro blood, does not diminish at all; it rather increases.

This fanaticism is not the least evil feature in the African Arab; it becomes in many cases a merciless hatred towards Christians, justifying any robbery, **Fanaticism.** cruelty, or outrage. It is this spirit, combined with degeneracy of character, that reduces Morocco to misery, when it has all the elements of prosperity. As Hooker and Ball say (in " A Tour in Morocco "), " over the provinces wherein they are able to enforce it, the rule of the Moorish Sultans is little else than an organised system of extortion, in which unchecked licence is given to the agents of the central authority. The springs of industry and enterprise are broken; no man can dream of improving his own condition or that of his family, unless by elaborate fraud or concealment he can hoard up wealth, which he dare not employ in any way useful to the community." The great need of the country is now, to pass under the control of some European power; even Spain could not be a worse master than the Arab.

Both Algeria and Morocco have many marabouts, or

RICH JEWESS OF TUNIS.

saints; entire tribes consist of so-called descendants of the Prophet. While very many Arabs of Algeria still live as nomad shepherds, in Morocco **Physical characters.** they are mostly sedentary and sociable, living in villages and associating for meals in the mosque or the tent which replaces it. In Algeria their long narrow faces display their very evident finesse, though they try to hide it under the mask of impassiveness. Their features are often markedly Jewish and Caucasian; but their thin muscular bodies, brown complexion, black fiery eyes, straight black hair, and thin beard give them sufficiently distinctive characteristics. Their women are relatively short and slightly made.

The Arabs of the towns, mixed to a considerable extent with Berbers and other foreigners, are known as Moors. They are diminishing, but still form an im- **Arabs of the towns.** portant element in the population of Algeria. The Arabs flourish most as nomads on the highlands, untamable, unteachable. They do not take kindly to agriculture, but love riding, camping out, hunting, shepherding. Left to themselves, they are hospitable and magnanimous; when their hostility is roused, it is implacable.

Taking Tunis as an example of a North African city, it may be described as a large walled town divided into quarters for different classes of inhabitants. **The city of Tunis.** Its streets are remarkable for tortuosity and irregularity. Many houses on opposite sides of the streets are connected by arcades, on which sometimes a couple of storeys are built. Sometimes these connecting links form long galleries. Often the houses have rich marble columns and walls with Moorish sculptures or designs. The trade quarter is a labyrinth of streets devoted to special occupations; often the merchandise is manufactured on the spot, and cloth-making, wool-combing, copper-beating, dyeing, and many other processes may be seen by the passer-by. The Tunisian "upper ten" and the Moors live in a special quarter, the Bab-es-Souika, and do their best to render Tunis an African Paris. They dress well, affecting choice colours, pale blue, pink, cream; but the ladies are too stout for elegance, and are not so choice in costume as the men, to say nothing of their black veils with narrow openings. The poor sometimes wear a simple burnouse of grey wool or brown stuff with white embroidery. Their numbers are increased by emigration from Algeria and Morocco. The Jews,—nearly one-third of the population,—have their special quarter; and the various European settlers congregate mainly together. But Tunis, though so proud of being Europeanised, has not reformed its scavenging. The streets are unlit after sunset, and are likewise unpaved; and the odours surpass those of Cologne in the worst days.

For many reasons the sacred city of Kairwan, in the interior of Tunis, is far more highly esteemed than that of Tunis. It has a very fine mosque, and formerly neither Jews nor Christians were allowed to come near it. It is a great resort of pilgrims, who call it one of the four gates of paradise, and say that seven days of Kairwan are equal to one day in Mecca, and confer the title of Hadji. It was not till 1881, when the French took it, that any Christians entered the mosque.

Jews, though despised, flourish in large numbers in the towns of Northern Africa. Tetuan is one of their headquarters, and many of the Jews of Morocco are descended from those who were at different times expelled from Spain and Portugal. They have a large part of the trade of North Africa in their hands. Very often they, especially the women, display a tendency to corpulence. This is also notable in the Tunis Jews, who belong to two groups, the Italian, dressing like Europeans, and the Spanish, who dress like Moors, excepting the women, who do not veil, and wear pointed caps embroidered with gold. The Algerian Jews, mainly Spanish, are becoming largely assimilated to the French. Strange to say, many of the undoubted Jews of Tunis, having adopted Mahometanism when subjected to persecution, retain their faith now they are free. The mass of the Tunis Jews read the Pentateuch and pray in Hebrew, and retain a singular relic of ancient feuds in a prayer that God will " pour out his anger upon Spain, as well as on Ishmael (the Arab), Kedar (all kinds of Mussulmans), and Edom (Christians)." They are however peaceable, skilful traders and sharp bargainers. They are increasing rapidly. The girls were formerly, it is said, specially dieted to make them fat. They were not considered respectable-looking until their arms and legs were stout enough to wear very large rings and bracelets. It must be added that the Tunis Jews are less moral than nearly all their race, and are even worse than their neighbours in that respect.

As to the products, industries, and commerce of Northern Africa, it is to be hoped that in another quarter of a century much more may be said than can be *Products and* now. Good leather still comes from Morocco, *industries.* and Fez retains a large manufacture of red caps and scarves. Morocco also carries on a considerable caravan trade with the interior of the Sahara and tropical Africa. In Algeria the growth of esparto grass and halfa for paper-making, of the eucalyptus, of cotton, of wheat, and of tobacco, is being largely promoted. Both Morocco and Algeria have a rich future in store when their mineral wealth is developed. The fisheries of Tunis, especially tunny-fishing, are valuable, as also is the coral dredging, producing coral to the value of several hundred thousands a year.

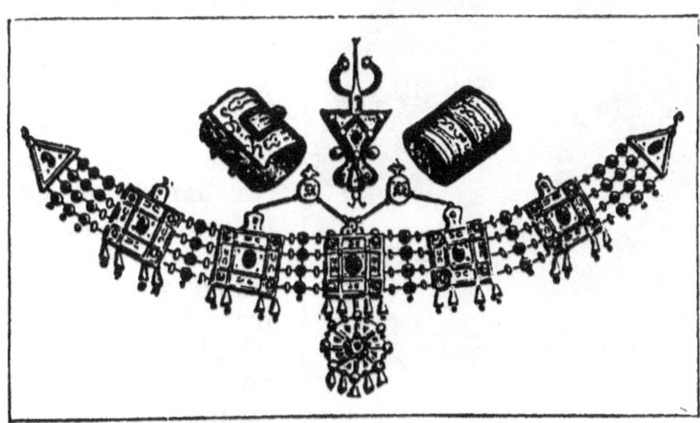

ORNAMENTS OF KABYLE WOMEN.

CHAPTER III.
The Nubians and Abyssinians.

Ethiopia—The early Abyssinians—Intercourse with Jews and Greeks—Kingdom of Axum—Conversion to Christianity—Isolation by Mahometans—
Portuguese missions—The Gallas—King Theodore's career—The English
expedition—The Uaua of Nubia—Christian kingdom of Dongola—The
Egyptians in Nubia—The Nubian negroes—Physical character—Dress—
Moral character—Houses and trade—The Bisharis—Physical and moral
character—The Ababdeh—The Agau of Abyssinia—The Basé—Their character—The Jews or Felashas—The Bogos—The Changallas—The people
of Tigré—Bruce's travels—Raw beef banquets—Women feeding the men
—Marriage—Religion—Number of churches — The Abuna—Superstitions
—Houses—Government—Agriculture and industry—Languages.

NUBIAN.

"ETHIOPIA" was once the prevalent name for the regions of Africa inhabited by "black people," so far Ethiopia. as known to the ancients. As knowledge progressed, the term became limited, until it can hardly be said now to extend farther than Abyssinia properly so called, a name derived from the Arabic name "Habesch," mixture or confusion, from the mixed character of the people. The Abyssinians call themselves "Itiopiavian" or Ethiopians.

Cut.off though they were in their mountainous country by tracts very difficult to traverse, the Abyssinians early had communication with Egypt, and were sometimes under the same monarch. It is claimed, too, **The early** by the Abyssinians, that the Queen of Sheba **Abyssinians.** who visited Solomon was one of their queens; and that from her son by him their royal line is descended. Fur- thermore, after the dispersion of the Jews by Assyrian conquests, many of them settled in Abyssinia, **Intercourse** which indicates that they already had con- **with Jews** siderable knowledge of and intercourse with **and Greeks.** the country. Later, the Greeks reached Abyssinia in the time of the Ptolemies, and founded colonies, and left various traces of their presence. The kingdom **Kingdom of** of Axum rose to considerable power in the **Axum.** second century A.D.; and the ruins of the city of Axum still show its former greatness. The ruins of Adulis, once its sea-port on the Red Sea, are now four miles inland, as the result of the silting up of the Red Sea.

The early Christians knew enough of Abyssinia to seek to conquer it for their faith; and Athanasius of Alexan- dria, about A.D. 330, consecrated Frumentius **Conversion to** to be the first bishop for Abyssinia. Well pre- **Christianity.** pared by their acquaintance with Judaism, the Abyssinians adopted Christianity; and in the fifth century a large number of monks settled in the country, and the monastic system grew powerful and still flourishes. In the next century, the Abyssinian king conquered Yemen in Arabia, at the request of the emperor Justinian; and the Abyssin- ians traded widely to India, Ceylon, and Southern Europe. The Mahometan advance, however, shut them **Isolation by** once more within their old territory. About **Mahometans.** 960 a Jewess murdered all the royal family but an infant; and she and her descendants reigned over the country for 300 years, when the old dynasty recovered power.

About the end of the fifteenth century the Portuguese commenced their celebrated missions to Abyssinia, under- taken with the idea of discovering a traditional Christian

monarch in the East, known as Prester John.   The Portu-
Portuguese guese were able to give the Abyssinians consider-
missions. able assistance against the Arabs, when they invaded their country in the sixteenth century ; but they
afterwards quarrelled with them, on the question of alle-

giance to Rome among others, and finally they were
expelled in 1633.

During the middle of the sixteenth century, the Gallas
The Gallas. from the south began to encroach on Abyssinia,
and finally gained great influence in the country,
practically controlling the "Negus," as the emperor or king

is styled. In the present century, numerous English missionaries entered Abyssinia, and were followed by naturalists and politicians. King Theodore, whose career has become so well-known through the British expedition in 1868, was born in 1818, and was not of royal but of noble descent; and by successive stages of rebellion and fighting, rose from an inferior position to be king in 1855. At this time he is described as a man of education and intelligence, a born ruler, of majestic bearing, very generous, and by no means greedy or lustful, but liable to extreme outbursts of anger and pride, with fanatical religious zeal. He was also "the best shot, the best spearman, the best runner, and the best horseman in Abyssinia." But unfortunately he tried to subdue the Gallas, a task beyond his strength; still he took their stronghold of Magdala, which he made his capital, and gained over many of their chiefs. He conquered the kingdom of Shoa in the south, but by this time heavy taxation and war levies were exhausting the people; and his second marriage not proving happy, Theodore gave himself up to drinking and immorality. But English neglect of a letter which Theodore had sent to Queen Victoria in response to a present, is largely responsible for our subsequent difficulties with him. He kept several of our envoys prisoners for years, during which his government grew more oppressive, and numerous portions of his kingdom rebelled. At last the English expedition was sent; and after a war, in which Theodore showed much military and engineering skill, Magdala was taken, and Theodore was found dead by his own hand. The present king of Abyssinia, Johannes, was formerly governor of Tigré, and aided the English expedition greatly.

Nubia, although not strictly definable as a country, may be taken to include the valley of the Nile from Assouan to Khartoum, and the country on either side from the Red Sea to the Libyan desert. It was included by the early Egyptians in Ethiopia. The people then inhabiting the country were negroes, called Uaua by the Egyptians as far back as the sixth dynasty,

ABYSSINIAN WATER-GIRLS.

and down to the time of the Ptolemies. During the Roman possession of Egypt, the negroes began to be pressed upon by the ancestors of the present Beja or Bishari

BENI AMER WARRIORS.

tribes ; and the emperor Diocletian, in withdrawing all Roman troops above the cataracts, authorised the Nobatæ, who were kindred people to the Uaua, and came from Kordofan, to repel the attacks of these Hamitic invaders.

E

But the latter were too strong, and the result was an intermingling, followed in the sixth century by the conversion of the Nubians to Christianity.

A Christian kingdom of Nubia was founded at Dongola, and from it were driven the Hamites who refused to be **Christian** converted; and this kingdom long withstood **kingdom of** the Arab Mahometans, who gained control of **Dongola.** lower Nubia. It was not overthrown till the fourteenth century, when the Arabs gained the help of a small army of Bosnians sent by the Turkish Sultan Selim. These Bosnians settled in Nubia and mingled with the natives and the Arabs, giving to many of their descendants a light complexion. The people became **The** Mahometans, and the Mahdi of recent history **Egyptians** was a native of Dongola. The Egyptians un- **in Nubia.** der Turkish rule subjugated Nubia in 1822, but have again lost nearly the whole of it as a consequence of the ill-advised and evanescent conquest of the regions above the cataracts.

Negroes, Arabs, and Hamites make up the present population of Nubia. The negroes term themselves Barabra **The Nubian** or Berberins, but have scarcely the slightest **negroes.** affinity with the true Berbers of Chapter II. They are in fact among the darkest of African negroes, **Physical** sometimes almost black, but with a reddish **character.** tint, and have long heads, very wavy or woolly hair, large but well-shaped lips, and large black eyes. The features are very regular, but the nose is larger than in most negroes, although straight and strong-looking, while the cheek-bones are less prominent. Their teeth are very white and small. They usually disfigure themselves with three oblique scars on each cheek; and not unfrequently they voluntarily inflict wounds on themselves, a supposed means of curing diseases.

Their dress is a tunic, and over it a blue cotton robe. Sandals are of course worn, and sometimes a turban **Dress.** Most of them carry weapons, concealed if not openly, at least a knife or a dagger. The girls wear little beyond a girdle or apron decked with pearls, and sometimes with gold and silver ornaments. They wear nose-rings, and usually bits of wood in the lobes of their ears, replacing them when married by gold or silver. The married women dress more completely, enveloping themselves in a loose robe, and dress their hair as elaborately as is depicted on the Egyptian monuments, with regular curls stiffened by fat and ochre, and sometimes covered with thick layers of gum.

The Nubian negroes are hard-working agriculturists, and in many ways superior to the Egyptians, being more self-dependent and self-defensive, and honest **Moral** and cheerful. Many of them have emigrated **character.** to Egypt, and have taken service in Cairo as porters, domestic servants, artisans, etc. These rising emigrants can usually read and write Arabic, and are capable of reckoning. It is doubtful whether Egyptian domination did much for their country, and whether it will not do better now that it is relieved from the exactions of the late rulers.

The Nubians have few large collections of houses, and their dwellings are often mere mud-huts, with conical or square roofs, having a courtyard outside, pro- **Houses and** tected by a wall. Very few things are manu- **trade.** factured or exported, but a considerable transit trade goes on, by which gold, ostrich feathers, ivory, and slaves are transported from Central Africa towards Asiatic and European markets. The Dongola Nubians live chiefly at and near Dongola and on the islands in the river, and are by far the most commercial. They are also settled in considerable numbers at Khartoum, in Kordofan, and in Darfur. Altogether, these people may number a million and a half.

There are at least three main dialects of the Nubian language from Assouan to Meroe, though they have in no case become literary. There is no gender form, all harsh consonants are softened, and the verbs have a multiplicity of tense and mood forms. Nearly all speak Arabic.

The Beja, or Bishari, tribes of Eastern Nubia number perhaps only 200,000. They are of middle height, lean but muscular, and of great cunning. They are no doubt representatives of the so-called Hamitic people, and are very different from the negroes, though they have slightly mixed with them. Their predominant tint is reddish rather than black, and in the women the complexion approaches the swarthiness of southern Europe. They have strongly aquiline noses, very spare cheeks, with skin stretched over the cheek prominences, high foreheads, and abundance of tangled, not wavy or frizzly, hair. They do not smoke, and their teeth retain great whiteness. Their eyes are brilliant and expressive, but, owing to their desert life, they keep them half-closed. Altogether, they have a fierce and sinister appearance, and have been described as avaricious and pitilessly cruel. But they can talk in a lively fashion, and are gay and inquisitive. They are not very zealous followers of Islam, and have not a few pagan practices. With them property is common to the family or the tribe. Duelling is not uncommon, and is conducted by knife-strokes alternately given by the combatants, so as not to inflict mortal wounds. Among them are the Hadendowas and Amarars.

The Bisharis.

Physical and moral character.

The Ababdeh or Habab tribes, probably mixed Semites and Hamites, are not much more attractive than the Bisharis, though much fewer in number. Armed with long swords or lances, and enveloped in a great sheet of cotton cloth, used as a sleeping covering at night, they haunt the Nubian desert from Korosko to Abu Hamed. They do not live in tents, but have a sort of movable hut of wicker and straw, which the camels carry when they change their camp. They gain a better opinion from travellers than the Bisharis for truthfulness and frankness. The tribes known as Beni-Amer appear to be a mixture of Abyssinians and Bejas. Various Arab or half-Arab tribes, among whom the Kabbabish and the Hassanieh are the best known, complete the population of Nubia, numbering perhaps two or three hundred thousand.

The Ababdeh.

The Abyssinians really include several peoples and tribes of diverse origin, Hamitic, Semitic, and Negro, and

no one description is universally applicable. The Agau
of the west of Abyssinia perhaps represent The Agau of
the fundamental aboriginal type. They still Abyssinia.
retain ceremonies recalling early Egyptian religious practices. They worship the water of the Blue Nile, and also
venerate serpents. It is possible that they may be related to the Basé or Kunama of the Settite river (a tributary of the Atbara), who however would seem to have
some negro admixture. The Basé have very The Basé.
negro-like features, though their noses are not
flattened, nor are their lips very thick. Many of them
wear nothing but
a piece of skin
round the waist,
though some of
them wear a little
cotton cloth. One
of their peculiari-
ties is a mode of
"standing at
ease," by placing
the sole of the
right foot against
the left knee.
The women wear
plentiful supplies
of beads and
cowrie shells, with
nose-rings, and

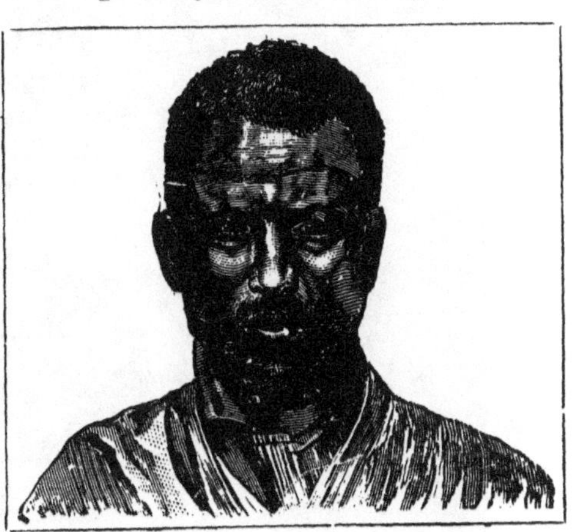

ABYSSINIAN.

some have anklets of skin. They make a sort of intoxi-
cant of dhurra grain, which, as well as water, they carry
in baskets of doum leaves so plaited as to be waterproof.
They have cooking pots, drinking gourds, and rough
wooden bedsteads in their beehive huts.

The Basé, though living in utterly separate villages,
without alliance among one another, are very formidable
to and untamable by the Arabs. No quarter Their
is given by them, and, as Sir S. W. Baker says character.
("Nile Tributaries of Abyssinia"), "the Basé cannot be
positively subdued; armed with the lance as their only

weapon, but depending upon extreme agility and the natural difficulties of their mountain passes, the attack of the Basé is always by stealth; their spies are ever prowling about unseen like the leopard, and their onset is invariably a surprise."   Their country abounds in large

ABYSSINIAN DEACON AND PRIEST.

animals, which afford plenty of food. They are com- plained of as treacherous; but Mr. F. L. James and party, who visited them in 1881–2 ("Wild Tribes of the Sou- dan"), found that it was possible by care and tact to get on well with them.

The Jews, or Felashas, of Ethiopia are old settlers very much resembling the Agau in features, both having their eyes a little oblique, and speaking a similar dialect. Though no longer having their former influence, they are tolerated and prosperous. Unlike The Jews, or Felashas.

ABYSSINIAN PRINCESS.

other Jews, they are not specially traders, but rather occupy themselves as artisans, and even as agriculturists and cattle-breeders. They keep the Sabbath strictly, offer frequent sacrifices, wash frequently, and isolate the diseased. They only marry among themselves, when of adult age, and have but one wife. They have a good character for morals.

The Bogos tribe, of the northern Abyssinian mountains of Senhit or Sennaheit, appear to be another group related to the Agau. They have been almost **The Bogos.** exterminated by attacks from Abyssinians on the one hand and Arabs on the other; but they are well worth study, having preserved many ancient customs. Thus, they are divided into two extremely separate castes —the elders, or patrons, and the clients; the latter possibly the descendants of captured or subject enemies. The client is a serf, but cannot be sold; he goes with the land, and has a right to the protection of his patron. The youngest son of the aristocrat inherits the ancestral abode, while the eldest son has the double-edged sword of his father, his lands, his serfs, and his white kine. Women do not inherit, and are treated as so much property, without rights and without responsibility, yet their person is protected from outrage. The husband never sees the face of his mother-in-law, nor does he pronounce her name; nor may the wife repeat the name of her husband or her father-in-law.

There are specimens of numerous tribes or people in Abyssinia of varying Arab, Hamitic, and Negro relationship, which we cannot fully particularise. Among those **The Changallas.** largely of negro blood are the Changallas of the western slope of the mountains. They are very dark in complexion, and still in a very barbarous state. The Arab traders, and even the Abyssinians, hunt among them for slaves, and they are naturally very hostile to all intruders.

Even among the mass of the Abyssinians, notable contrasts are to be observed. The people of Tigré, or the **The people of Tigré.** Tigritians, of the north-east are the most typical, and are distinguished by their long, narrow skulls and regular features. Their foreheads are high, their noses straight or somewhat aquiline, their lips thick, their eyes bright and resembling the Arabs, their hair wavy, their chins pointed. They have scanty beards, prominent cheek-bones, and good figures. In the eastern province of Lasta they have small heads and figures ana a comparatively light complexion, and are both bright-mannered and acute. The southern people of Amhara, Shoa, etc., are much darker, and are undoubtedly mixed with foreign elements. Their skulls are broad, their cheek-bones high, their eyes large, and their general expression pleasing. The hair, too, is curly, not to say wavy. These people are very hospitable and obliging, yet vain and braggart, and the men are particularly idle, leaving everything possible to the women.

James Bruce was the first great modern traveller who penetrated Abyssinia (1770–1772), and his travels give entertaining and marvellous pictures of Abyssinian life at that time. His stories of their eating raw **Bruce's travels.** beef were at first disbelieved, but have been abundantly confirmed. He thus describes one of their remarkable banquets. " A long table is set in the middle of a large room, and benches beside it for a **Raw beef banquets.** number of guests who are invited. A cow or bull, one or more, as the company is numerous, is brought close to the door, and his feet strongly tied. The skin that hangs down under his chin and throat is cut only so deep as to arrive at the fat, and by the separation of a few small bloodvessels, six or seven drops of blood only fall upon the ground. Having satisfied the Mosaical law, according to their conception, by pouring these six or seven drops upon the ground, two or more of them fall to work. On the back of the beast, and on each side of the spine, they cut skin deep ; then putting their fingers between the flesh and the skin, they begin to strip the hide of the animal half-way down his ribs, and so on to the buttock, cutting the skin wherever it hinders them commodiously to strip the poor animal bare. All the flesh on the buttock is cut off then, and in solid, square pieces, without bones or much effusion of blood ; and the prodigious noise the animal makes is a signal for the company to sit down to table.

" There are then laid before every guest, instead of plates, round cakes, if I may so call them, about twice as big as a pancake, and something thicker and tougher,

It is unleavened bread of a sourish taste, far from being
disagreeable, and very easily digested, made of a grain
called teff.   It is of different colours, from black to the
colour of the whitest wheat-bread.   Two or three servants
then come, each with a square piece of beef in their bare
hands, laying it upon the cakes of teff, placed like dishes
down the table, without cloth or anything else beneath
them.   By this time all the guests have knives in their
hands, and the men have their large crooked ones, which
they put to all sorts of uses during the time of war.
The company are so ranged that one man sits between
two women; the man with his long knife cuts a thin piece

ABYSSINIAN WOMAN.

which would be thought a good
beef-steak in England, while you
see the motion of the fibres yet
perfectly distinct, and alive in the
flesh.   No man in Abyssinia, of
any fashion whatever, feeds himself, or touches his own meat.   The
women take the steak
and cut it lengthways
like strings, about the
thickness of your little finger, then
crossways into square pieces, something smaller than dice.   This
they lay upon a piece of the teff
bread, strongly powdered with
black pepper, or Cayenne pepper,
and fossil-salt, they then wrap it up in the teff bread like
a cartridge.

"In the mean time, the man having put up his knife,
with each hand resting upon his neighbour's knee, his
body stooping, his head low and forward, and mouth
open like an idiot, turns to the one whose cartridge is
first ready, who stuffs the whole of it into his mouth,
which is so full that he is in constant danger of being
choked.   This is a mark of grandeur.   The greater a
man would seem to be, the larger piece he takes in his
mouth; and the more noise he makes in chewing, the
more polite he is thought to be.   They have indeed a

proverb that says, 'Beggars and thieves only eat small pieces, or without making a noise.' Having despatched this morsel, which he does very expeditiously, his next female neighbour holds forth another cartridge, which goes the same way; and so on till he is satisfied. He never drinks till he has finished eating; and before he begins, in gratitude to the fair ones that fed him, he makes up two small rolls of the same kind and form; each of his neighbours open their mouths at the same time, while with each hand he puts their portions into their mouths. He then falls to drinking out of a large handsome horn; the ladies eat till they are satisfied, and then all drink together."

Marriage, Bruce described as a mere temporary arrangement in Abyssinia, and it appears that **Marriage.** a priest's aid is rarely called in. Once he was present in a company where there was pointed out to him a woman of high rank among them, and seven men who had been her husbands, none

ABYSSINIAN.

of whom was the husband at that time. On separation, they divide the children, the eldest son falling to the mother, the eldest daughter to the father. Burial in churchyards is practised, and funeral masses and feasts follow death.

Religiously, the Abyssinians are Christians by profession, in spite of the propagandism of Mahometanism in their neighbourhood. Taking origin at a time **Religion.** when Christianity was still in a somewhat indeterminate state, the Abyssinian Church preserves a singular crudity of ideas. They belong specially to the division of Christians called "monophysite," regarding

Christ as possessed only of one nature, and the Holy Ghost as proceeding from God the Father only. But there is no doubt that, according to their lights, the

Abyssinians are a religious nation. "There is no country in the world," says Bruce, "where there are so many churches as in Abyssinia. Though the country is very

mountainous, and consequently the view much obstructed, it is very seldom you see less than five or six churches, and, if you are on a commanding ground, five times that number. Every great man that dies, thinks he has atoned for all his wickedness if he leaves a fund to build a church, or has built one in his lifetime. The situation of a church is always chosen near running water, for the convenience of their purifications and ablutions, in which they observe strictly the Levitical law." The churches are full of slovenly pictures of saints, but there are no statues or sculptures.

Numbers of churches.

The chief of the Church is called the Abuna, that is, " Our father," and for several centuries has always been a foreigner, a Coptic priest (with which primitive Church they are in communion) sent by the Patriarch of Alexandria. But he has very little power, though he ordains priests and deacons. These latter, as well as monks, are in great numbers in Abyssinia. The monks, however, do not live in convents, but in houses round the churches, and they cultivate land. They are very much given to ceremonials, too numerous and complex for us here to describe. Their morals are not too highly spoken of. Circumcision is practised, as among the Jews.

The Abuna.

It is a strange custom in Abyssinia for men to leave the house when the women are in childbirth. After birth the infant is carried to a window, a man passes a lance in from outside, and the point is put into the child's mouth. The women then make loud outcries, twelve for a boy, three for a girl, and then pursue the men, who, when caught, have to provide presents, generally of food or drink.

It may be due to the neighbourhood and admixture of negro ideas, that the Abyssinians, in spite of their Christianity, have so many superstitions. A demon called Bonda is supposed to haunt blacksmiths, enabling them at will to appear as animals, especially hyenas, or to transform and enchant other people. The Bonda has an evil reputation for robbing graves. Another kind of evil spirit they believe in can only be driven out

Superstitions.

by music, of the noisiest description and long protracted. Another strange practice is, for a woman who has lost two or three children by death, to cut off the tip of her left ear, wrap it in bread, and swallow it. This is done in the hope that it will save the life of another infant just born.

Abyssinian houses are usually circular, though some are square, with flat roofs. Some have numerous rooms, but there is little separation between the family and the horses. Tables and seats are used, and arms and trappings deck the walls.

Houses.

The number and power of the district chiefs, called "Ras," are a great barrier to the power of the king or emperor. Each village, too, has its separate head or "shum," with very little real responsibility to the king. There is a book of law called the "Guide of Rulers," supposed to be Byzantine in origin, a mixture of regulations drawn partly from the Pentateuch, partly from the code of the Emperor Justinian, which gives the father absolute rights over his son, and imposes heavy penalties on all offences. Mutilations and tortures are common punishments. There are numerous kinds of capital punishment, and these are carried out immediately after condemnation of the offenders. The Abyssinians are very litigious, in addition to their well-known fighting propensities, and their vanity is extraordinary. One traveller says he believes the chief mental employment of the lowest fellows in the country, is building castles in the air, and imagining how they would act and what they would say if they were great men.

Government.

Agriculture is in a very low state in this disturbed country. The ploughshares are little better than sticks or lances. The ground is not hoed or tended during the growth of the crops. Gum, which might be largely gathered, is almost neglected. The land is naturally fertile, and in some parts is said to furnish five crops a year; but it is ill cultivated. War and plunder being so common, industrial arts have received little attention, and have been left to the Felashas and to foreigners. Perhaps the work in which Abyssinians

Agriculture and industry

most excel is the preparation of leather, and its manufacture into shields, saddles, amulets, etc. The religious body has some good copyists and illuminators of manuscripts. Flattering bards are often kept by the chiefs.

The Tigritians speak a language derived from the Geez, the old Semitic language still in use in the Abyssinian Church, though no longer under- Languages. stood by the people. The Tigritian language has also many words from aboriginal sources in Abyssinia, and others from the Galla (Hamitic) language. The Amharic, another language derived from the Geez, is now gaining ground, and is most used in trade and at court. It has a special alphabet of 33 letters, each with seven forms, giving 231 forms to be acquired. The language is written from left to right, unlike Hebrew and Arabic. The British Museum has a large collection of works in Amharic.

Massowah, the chief port of Northern Abyssinia, has received much notice through its recent as well as its past history. It is situated upon a small coral island connected with the land by piers, and was in the sixteenth century taken by the Turks, who, failing to conquer Abyssinia, withdrew. Then the Hababs, mingled with the Turkish Bosnian garrison, chose a naïb, or governor, who at first received a subsidy from the Turks, but they were afterwards compelled to acknowledge the sovereignty of the Abyssinians. Not till 1866 was the nominal authority of the Turks exchanged for that of the Egyptians. They have now given way to the Italians who may achieve something considerable in the development of the Red Sea trade and of relations with Abyssinia. Massowah is one of the hottest places in the world, the thermometer frequently reaching 100° F. in the shade in winter. But a great trade has been carried on there by the Banyans or Hindu Mahometan merchants; and after the interruptions caused by the recent hostile attitude of the Abyssinians to the Italians have ceased, it will probably increase largely. It has a number of considerable stone buildings and houses, Arab in style, while many of the inhabitants live in huts made of leafy branches.

CHAPTER IV.
The Gallas, Somalis, etc.

The Gallas—Physical characters—Dress and weapons—Cattle-breeding—Religion—The Latookas—The Danakil, or Afer—The Somali—Cattle-breeding — Commerce — Language and morals — Marriage—Life in a chief's house — Meals — Burton's journey to Harar — The Harari — Dress of women—Commerce—Furniture—The Socotrans.

IN the eastern horn of Africa the Gallas and Somalis are an important group of people, extending considerably into Abyssinia, and into what was recently the Egyptian Soudan. They have only become clearly known to Europeans in the last quarter of a century; but it is now pretty evident that they are mainly of the Hamitic, allied to the Semitic stock. To a large extent they are Mahometans.

The Gallas. The Gallas extend into southern Abyssinia, and largely inhabit the kingdom of Shoa, in the south-east of Abyssinia. King Menelik of Shoa has acknowledged the supremacy of King John of Abyssinia, but has been largely extending his sway over the Gallas. The extensive country south of Abyssinia is still very little known. The main country of the Gallas is west of the river Juba.

Some authors are inclined to lay most stress on the darkness of complexion and the wavy hair and rather thick lips of the Gallas, and to regard them **Physical** as largely negroes. Others regard them as **characters.** Semites, or even as Aryans, whose darkness is due to their place of residence. There is no question that they are finely formed, with expressive eyes, and broad and high brows; their skulls are long (dolichocephalic). The general set of their muscles has little in common with the negroes. They appear to have considerable affinity with the Agau of Abyssinia. The men vary from a reddish to a deep brown, the women are even sometimes fair in complexion, and are mostly good-looking. **Dress and** Both sexes wear the Abyssinian mantle. Only **weapons.** those who have earned the distinction by killing a man, may, in many tribes, wear a special head-dress, and an ostrich's feather. Lances, shields of skin, and double-edged knives are the Galla weapons. Their houses are conical structures, thatched with grass or reeds, and resting on circles of stones.

Although a warlike and rather exclusive race of nomads, the Gallas are intelligent and open to new ideas beyond most of their neighbours. They are said to **Cattle-** show considerable facility in learning new **breeding.** languages. In cattle-breeding they are pre-eminent, seven or eight beasts being possessed for every human being; some have large numbers of horses; others keep many hives of bees. Being still in a tribal state, their organization leads to constant warfare, and a vendetta is maintained with great cruelty and inveteracy. Galla captives have been known to die of hunger, rather than work for their masters; but the children are often sold into slavery by the chiefs. Yet women have a comparatively high position among them. One wife is the rule and women may refuse an unacceptable match.

The majority of the Gallas have become Mahometans. A few tribes in the North have become Christianised, some by Roman Catholics, others by Protestants. **Religion.** A large portion of the people remains pagan, believing, however, in one supreme God, whom they call

Waka, to whom they pray for rain and for victory; but they sacrifice to other subordinate deities. At the beginning of the rainy season they sacrifice to the male deity; at the harvest time to the goddess of fruitfulness. They venerate every living thing and imposing natural phenomena; every family having its protecting tree. In the North there are priests and sorcerers, who pretend to decide the future, and charm evil spirits away.

The Latookas. The Latookas, extending almost to the Nile, appear to be related to the Gallas: Sir Samuel Baker ("Albert N'yanza") is enthusiastic about their

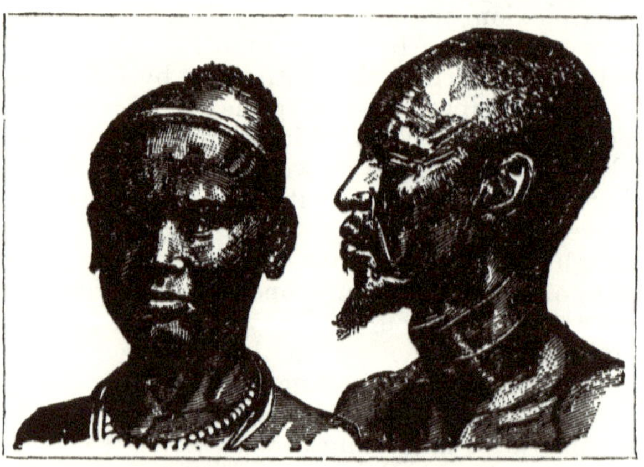

GALLA BOY.　　　　　　　SOMALI.

fine physique; like that of the Gallas, the average height of the men, he says, reaching five feet eleven and a half inches. Their general behaviour is very cheerful, though they are always ready to fight. They have large collections of cattle, which are watched day and night by sentinels on high platforms.

The Latooka men are entirely naked; their great pride is in their head-dress, which requires a long time to perfect. The women are plain-looking, but massive and powerful. They wear a small apron of leather in front, and a long artificial tail, like that of a horse, behind.

Their hair is worn short, and dressed with red ochre and grease. They have largely lost any religion they may have had, and Sir Samuel Baker says they have not even a superstition upon which to found a religious feeling.

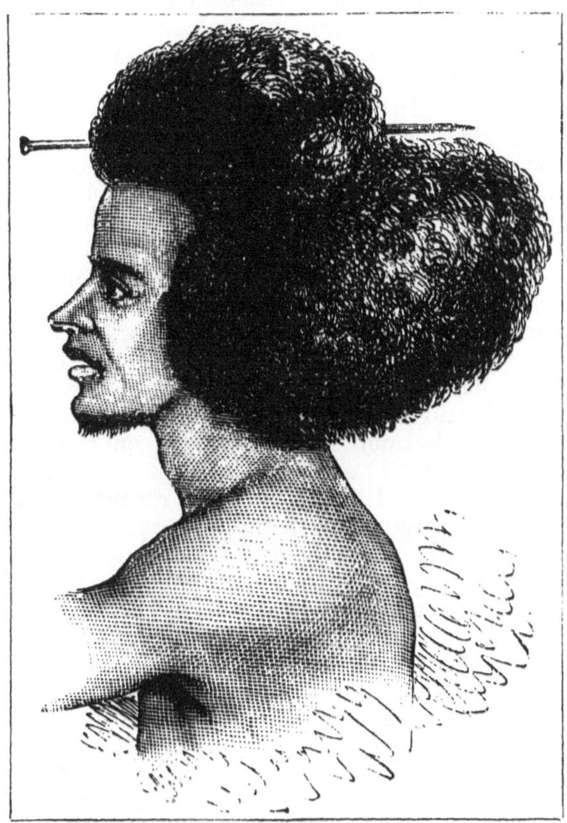

MAHOMED, A DANAKIL.

Although very non-moral and practising polygamy, they are capable of some industrial arts, being good blacksmiths, though they have to use stones for hammers and anvils.

The Danakil, or Afer, inhabiting the country directly East of Abyssinia, extending to the Red Sea, though **The Danakil,** calling themselves Arabs, and probably consider- **or Afer.** ably intermixed with them, speak a Hamitic language, and are in many respects like the Gallas and Somalis. Although nominally Mahometans, they retain many pagan beliefs and practices. They are finely formed people, and the young women, who are never veiled, are quite beautiful; but later in life their hard out-of-door work, and the hot, dry climate, soon deprive them of their good looks. Both sexes wear a waist cloth of many coloured cloths, and a sort of mantle, or an animal's skin thrown over the shoulder. The men wear a porcupine's quill in their head-dress, and when they have killed an enemy, proudly wear an ostrich's feather. Their numerous tribes combine or separate on slight grounds, and have hereditary chiefs, known, as in Abyssinia, by the title of Ras, who execute the will of the majority. Their chief support is derived from taking toll of caravans, which they protect and guard, but sometimes plunder. Some of them are fishermen and navigators on the Red Sea, formerly indulging in piracy. It is partly within their territories that the Italians have in recent years established trading settlements on the Red Sea.

From below the Equator and the mouth of the River Juba, northwards, and in the easternmost part of Africa, **The Somalis.** north and east of the River Juba, the Somali are the dominant and very numerous people. They are physically a fine race, whom many observers describe as very handsome, with oval faces, high rounded foreheads, full lips, strong regular teeth, and bright eyes. Like the Gallas they certainly have a considerable tincture of negro blood; they are very dark brown, and their hair approaches the frizzly type. They often have long hair plucked into tresses hanging to the shoulders. Their usual costume is a mantle thrown over the shoulder.

The Somali are divided into a great number of tribes and clans, whose names it would be profitless to mention. They are for the most part warlike and fanatical Mahometans, and carry spears, shields, and short swords, like the ancient Egyptians, using their weapons readily in disputes. They lead for the most part a nomad life, though many are settled in towns. Many are cattle-breeders, others agriculturists, growing the duhrra grain and collecting frankincense and myrrh. Berberah and Zeyla, their principal ports on the Red Sea (now under British protection, together with a large tract of the coast of north-eastern Africa), carry on a considerable trade with Egypt, Arabia, and India, exporting gums, hides, ostrich feathers, and coffee : most of the trade is in the hands of Hindu traders. The Issa are a powerful tribe among them, acting as caravan-protectors, or as carriers by camel. Their wives accompany them everywhere, leading the camels, carrying wood, utensils, and probably a baby on their back. *Cattle-dreebing. Commerce.*

The language of the Somali is essentially Hamitic, and like that of the Gallas and Danakil. They are great talkers, quick-tempered, very susceptible to ridicule. Their morals cannot be described as elevated. Sir Richard Burton ("First Footsteps in East Africa") describes the women as very prolific, but peculiarly bad mothers, neither loved nor respected by their children. None will marry cousins. Marriages and portions are settled by relatives; a cloth, and a bead necklace, or a varying number of sheep, may be the portion. The bridegroom's first meeting his wife on marriage is celebrated by giving her a horse-whipping to tame her. Polygamy is very usual, and daughters are very frequently sold. Divorce is very common. Kissing is entirely unknown. Children run about naked, "eat as much as they can beg, borrow, or steal, and grow up healthy, strong, and well-proportioned." *Language and morals. Marriage.*

Life in a settled village of the Somali is thus described by Burton. Entering the cottage of the chief, you find a space divided by dwarf walls of wattle and dab into three compartments, for the men, women, and cattle. The horses and asses are tethered at night on the left of the door ; the wives lie on the right, near a large fireplace of stones and clay, and the males occupy the part opposite to and farthest from *Life in a Chief's house.*

the entrance. " The thatched ceiling shines jetty with smoke, which when intolerable is allowed to escape by a diminutive window; this seldom happens, for smoke, like grease and dirt, keeping man warm, is enjoyed by savages. Equally simple is the furniture : the stem of a tree, with branches hacked into pegs, supports the shields; the assegais are planted against the wall; and divers bits of wood, projecting from the sides and the central roof-tree of the cottage, are hung with clothes and other articles that attract white ants. Gourds smoked inside, and coffee cups of coarse black Harar pottery, with deep wooden platters, and prettily carved spoons of the same material, compose the household furniture. Long before dawn, the good wife rises, wakens her hand-maidens, lights the fire, and prepares for the morning meal. A flat smooth oval slab, weighing about fifteen pounds, and a stone roller six inches in diameter, worked with both hands, and the weight of the body kneeling ungracefully upon it on all fours, are used to triturate the holcus grain. At times water must be sprinkled over the meal, until a finely-powdered paste is ready for the oven : thus several hours labour is required to prepare a few pounds of bread. About 6 a.m. there appears a substantial breakfast of roast beef and mutton, with scones of Jowari grain, the whole drenched in broth. Of the men, few perform any

Meals. ablutions, but all use the tooth-stick before sitting down to eat. After the meal some squat in the sun, others transact business, and drive their cattle to the bush till 11 a.m., the dinner hour. There is no variety in the repasts, which are always flesh and holcus; these people despise fowls, and consider vegetables food for cattle. During the day there is no privacy; men, women, and children enter in crowds. Throughout the day, the slave-girls are busied in grinding, cooking, and quarrelling with dissonant voices; the men have little occupation beyond chewing tobacco, chatting, and having their wigs frizzled by a professional coiffeur. In the evening the horses and cattle return home to be milked and stabled: this operation concluded, all apply themselves to supper with a will. They sleep but little, and sit deep into the night, trimming the fire, and conversing merrily over their cups of millet beer."

Burton's journey to Harar, 1854-5, was one among his many adventures characterized by great daring, for no European for centuries had penetrated thither, **Burton's** though it is little more than 200 miles from **journey to** Berberah. It is the ancient capital of Hadiyah, **Harar.** one of seven States constituting the former Arab empire of Zeyla. It had frequent conflicts with the Abyssinian kings, and at one time, in the sixteenth century, conquered a large part of their territory. The modern city of Harar is walled, but mean-looking, with narrow lanes, huge rubbish heaps, and packs of wretched dogs. The houses are flat-roofed sheds of two stories, with doors formed of a single plank, and holes for windows high above the ground. The chief houses have separate apartments for the women, and stand at the bottom of large courtyards. The Mahometans have made it a sacred city, and built many plain mosques and crowded graveyards in it; numerous Ulemas and Sheikhs teach Moslem learning in the Harari dialect, which includes a good deal that is Semitic.

The people are very mixed, but the prevailing type is not handsome, being much disfigured by disease, yellowish brown in complexion, with short stubbly **The Harari.** hair and beard, and large ill-made limbs. Costume is very varied; the better classes wear loincloths under their mantles, and the officials have white calico drawers. The women appear more numerous than the men, with small heads, regular profiles, straight noses, rather small mouths. They wear blue or brown cotton shirts with short arms, and sashes. Women of the upper class going out throw a blue sheet over the **Dress of** head, but are rarely veiled. Their hair, parted **women.** in the centre, is gathered into two large bunches below the ears, and covered with dark blue muslin, the ends meeting under the chin. A black satin ribbon is passed round the head at the junction of hair and skin. Young girls gather their long hair into a knot behind, and from this a group of short close plaits falls to the shoulder.

"Silver ornaments are worn only by persons of rank. The ear is decorated with Somali rings or red coral beads, the neck with necklaces of the same material, and the forearms with six or seven of the broad rings of buffalo and other dark horns prepared in western India. Finally, stars are tattooed upon the bosom, the eyebrows are lengthened with dyes, the eyes fringed with kohl, and the hands and feet stained with henna. The women, who have harsh and screaming voices, weave cotton thread, carry water, work in the garden, and sit and sell goods in the street. Most of their time they are chewing tobacco, and their loose behaviour frequently procures them a public flogging. Drinking is prevalent among all classes. The Somali in the city are held almost in serfdom. The Gallas occupy the country almost up to the city gates."

Harar is essentially a commercial city, taking toll for every donkey-load of goods passing through it. It is a **Commerce.** great halfway house between regions, and an emporium of slaves. Its coffee is first-rate, and the native tobacco is good. Safflower is largely grown, for export to Arabia for dyeing cotton shirts and staining the skin yellow. Tobes or mantles are largely woven at Harar of fine long-stapled cotton, and are of extreme durability, and as soft as silk.

"The furniture of a house at Harar is simple—a few skins, and in rare cases a Persian rug, stools, coarse mats, **Furniture.** and Somali pillows, wooden spoons and porringers shaped with a hatchet, finished with a knife, stained red, and brightly polished. The gourd is a conspicuous article, and worked inside and fitted with a cover of the same material, it serves as cup, bottle, pipe, and water-skin." Meat is largely eaten, chiefly beef, mutton, poultry, etc.; holcus is the chief grain.

Socotra, a large island 150 miles east of Cape Guardafui, annexed in 1886 by Great Britain, has a small mixed **The Socotrans.** population, largely Arab, with African and other elements. They used to be Nestorian Christians; but have lost much of their faith. They also practise the old South Arabian moon worship.

CHAPTER V.

The Waganda and the Eastern Soudanese.

The Waganda—Physical characters—Excess of women—Dress—Occupations—Food—Meals—Houses—Industries—Habits and customs—Marriage—Slave traffic—Government—King Mtesa—King Mwanga and Bishop Hannington—Punishments—Army and navy—Religion—Amusements—Language—Contrasting characteristics—The Wanyoro—The Akka—Peculiar gestures—The Monbuttu—King Munza's royal state—Cannibalism—Work and food—Albinos—The Niam-niam—Mode of hair-dressing—Weapons—Meat-eating—Cannibalism—Scattered dwellings—Chiefs—Manufactures—Musical tastes—Marriage—Beliefs—Language—The Bongo—Habits—Dress—Ornaments—Marriage—Dwellings—Smith work and smelting—Manufactures—Influence of Mahometans—Music and singing—Religious ideas—Burial—Treatment of the sick—Language—The Bari—Value of cattle—The Dinka—Clothing and ornaments—Food—Dwellings—Regard for animals—The Shillooks—Hair-dressing—Religious ideas—Darfur—The Fors—Kordofan—Mixture of people—Marriage—Morals—The Nubas—Dogolowis—Kababish and Baggaras—The Funj—Khartoum.

MITTU WOMAN.

WE will include in this chapter all the Soudanese peoples lately subject to Egyptian rule, together with the Niam-Niam and the Waganda.[1] The latter, The Waganda. dwelling on the north, north-west, and west of Lake Victoria Nyanza, form the most convenient starting-point. The Waganda, indeed, through their late king

[1] The prefixed syllables *u*, *wa*, are among the characteristics of the Bantu languages. Thus, *U-ganda* signifies country of the Ganda; *Wa-ganda*, the Ganda people.

Mtesa, became the most noted of central Africans. The equator divides the Uganda territory into two nearly equal portions. In this fertile land the banana is luxuriant, rain falls during every month, and the elevation of the country (from five to six thousand feet) makes the climate comparatively mild and equable. Through this country fine roads have been made and are well kept, and bridges and causeways cross the swamps. One of the best accounts of the country and people is that given by Messrs. Wilson and Felkin in "Uganda and the Egyptian Soudan."

In this country dwell the Waganda race; negroes, with short woolly hair. The men are above middle **Physical** height, muscular, and well made; the women **characters.** when young are not bad-looking, and have small hands and feet. Among them are scattered the Wahuma, a race of herdsmen, perhaps descended from the aboriginal Abyssinians or related to the Gallas. They are tall and handsome, with oval faces, thin lips, and straight noses. They are very exclusive, and speak a language of their own. Not a few albinos are to be found in the court, and in the houses of the great chiefs. Dwarfs, too, are by no means uncommon, and form a privileged class at court.

Uganda has perhaps five million people; and Mr. Wilson estimates that there are three-and-a-half times as **Excess of** many women as men, an excess known nowhere **women.** else. It is due to polygamy in excess, to the frequent fearful hand-to-hand battles, in which vast numbers of men are killed, and to the appropriation of the wives of conquered tribes, the men being put to death.

The Waganda are exceptionally strict about dress, clothing themselves completely when in public. The national **Dress.** costume is the mbugu, or bark cloth, worn by men as a loose robe, tied in a knot over the shoulder, the arms being left bare; the women fasten their cloth tightly round the body just under the armpits. Many wear turbans of calico or coloured handkerchiefs, and sandals of buffalo hide. The chiefs sometimes wear a fine skin robe over the mbugu. Foreign dress, especially

Arab and Turkish, has however been partially introduced, including caftans, trousers, stockings, and the red fez.

Fighting being a prime necessity, the Waganda are well supplied with arms, having long spears, large light

DANCE OF ALIAB WOMEN, UPPER NILE.

wooden shields, bows and arrows, the former very stiff, the latter much barbed; and also a consider- Occupations. able number 'of guns, mostly old-fashioned.

In agriculture, the regular instrument is a sort of heart-shaped hoe, fastened to a hook-shaped wooden handle three feet long. They have two kinds of axes, and long, curved, thin knives, all made from native ore.

Vegetable food is predominant among these people, the banana being the staple, and the sweet potato next in importance; but meat is eaten by those who can get it.

Food. The Waganda are ingenious cooks, having a way of cooking their bananas by steaming, water being poured under a banana leaf laid in the earthen pot they use, and so boiled. Meat also is baked or boiled tightly wrapped in banana leaves.

" The chiefs and upper classes of people generally eat with their families and head slaves. The meals are served

Meals. up in a large hut, the floor in the middle of the room being covered with a layer of banana leaves; on these the food is placed, and every one gathers round in a circle. The hands are first washed, either with water or with circular napkins, the size of small plates, cut out of the succulent stem of the banana; these napkins contain so much sap that no water is required. Then all fall to with their fingers. . . . The meal over, the hands are again washed, coffee is handed round, and pipes are produced. . . . The Waganda never drink during meals, but at the conclusion take large draughts of water or plantain wine." Fish are largely caught, with hooks and lines and fish-traps, by the islanders and shore people.

Uganda houses are superior to most negro dwellings, some of them being very large, and surrounded by a

Houses. fence of tall grass, with but one gateway. The houses are usually circular or dome-shaped, and thatched down to the ground. Tiger-grass stems form the ribs, and plaited grass fills up the interstices. There are no windows, so the inside is very dark; it also gets much blackened by soot. The chiefs have separate huts for sleeping, living, cooking, etc., the king's " palace," the most extensive building, being as much as ninety feet long.

The industrial arts of the Waganda are somewhat numerous; they make coarse and fine pottery, the latter

including black drinking bowls and tobacco pipes, bark-
Industries. cloth from the bark of a species of fig, basket-
work, mats, metal work, etc. Dandyism is
ministered to by beautiful walking-sticks, carried by all
the "upper ten." Skin dressing is carried to high perfec-
tion, both for robes and for sandals.

The Waganda are a strange mixture of civilized and
uncivilized. Completely clothed, they also wash fre-
Habits and quently, and do not anoint themselves with oil
customs. or fat; but they drink freely, and eat to excess.
All smoke tobacco of good quality. Many have beards;
but, unlike most negroes, they rarely dress the hair in
any special way, and usually shave it all off. Tattooing
is not practised at all; and mutilations of the ear, lips,
and teeth are even prohibited, and punishable by death.

Wives are bought; and the marriage bond is a very
loose one. The ordinary price of a wife is either three or
Marriage. four bullocks, six sewing needles, or a small
box of percussion caps. Chiefs are buried in
wooden coffins. The bodies of dead slaves, of whom they
own great numbers, are thrown into the bush, to be de-
voured by wild beasts and birds of prey. Property is
divided among a man's sons at his death, the wives (excepting his own mother) becoming the property of the
eldest son.

Slaves, unfortunately, are most important articles of
traffic in Uganda; for the Arab traders supply guns,
Slave traffic. ammunition, beads, cloth, etc., in exchange for
human beings and ivory, the supply of the
latter being on the decrease. Barter is the only mode of
sale, money not being in use. Four yards of unbleached
calico (one doti) constitute the standard of value, and two
doti will buy a cow. Cowries, in strings of a hundred,
form the small change.

The government of Uganda is a kind of feudal system,
the king being by no means all-powerful, but greatly
Government. controlled by a council, including three leading
chiefs who are practically owners of all the
country. When they agree upon any course, the matter
is decided; but sometimes they disagree, and a council

of lesser chiefs and sycopnants gives advice. The three
chiefs choose the king out of his predecessor's children,
but always choose a child, thus increasing their influence.
If they disagree about the choice, they go to war about it,
and the victor's candidate becomes king. The brothers
of the king are kept prisoners till he comes of age, and
are then burnt, all except two or three, who are left to
keep up the succession. The chiefs decide all matters of
law and justice; but there is no written law, only traditional " principles."

The kings of Uganda belong properly to the Wahuma
tribe; and although much mixed with negro blood, Mtesa
showed clearly enough his distinctness of race King Mtesa.
from his subjects. Mtesa was very ambitious,
and courted all Europeans out of whom he could get
anything, especially guns and ammunition. " He is a
thorough man of the world," wrote Mr. Wilson, " and
when he pleases can be as courteous and gentlemanly as
any of our own aristocracy. He takes an intelligent
interest in a wide range of subjects, and will discuss for
hours abstruse points in theology, political economy, or
philosophy. He is intensely fickle, and never knows his
own mind for two days together, and, like a spoilt child,
is always wanting a new toy. He is very superstitious;
and if he dreams of any of the gods of the country, he
takes it as an omen of ill, and immediately offers human
sacrifices, sometimes to the number of several hundreds,
to appease the anger of the offended deity." Mtesa was
at one time inclined to yield to Mahometan influences,
at another time he favoured Christian missions greatly;
but he was disturbed by the advent of Roman Catholics
after the Protestants had been known to him some time.
But Christianity was making considerable progress in
Uganda; a printing press had been set up, whence portions of the New Testament, hymns, prayers, etc., were
distributed in the native language. It became the fashion
to learn to read, and lads might be seen everywhere sitting and sprawling, all reading.

Near the end of 1884, unfortunately, Mtesa died. His
death was not followed by the usual carnival of blood and

plunder; and the new King Mwanga's brothers were not
killed. But Mwanga proved a weak, vain, and
vicious youth, passionate and suspicious, and
was roused by the conservative chiefs to attack
the Christians, from fear that white men were approaching to take away his kingdom. Numerous converts were
burnt, while singing their Christian hymns. The story
of the martyrdom of Bishop Hannington and his party
in 1885, after their successful passage through Masai
land, is fresh in memory.

After such a record, it is not surprising to hear that
the Waganda have a variety of modes of execution,
including beheading, strangling, bleeding to
death, etc. Theft is often punished by cutting
off the hand, ears, or nose. The stocks are reserved for
small offences.

The army is the pride of Uganda; indeed, every male
of sufficient strength is enrolled in it, and an army can
be collected sooner than anything else. In war
only a loin-cloth is worn, faces being whitened
with ashes to strike terror into the hearts of the enemy.
Being settled round so great a lake, naval skill has also
been acquired by the Waganda. They have a large fleet
of war-canoes, many of which will hold forty men.

Religiously, the Waganda, independently of Mahometanism and Christianity, are on a higher level than most
African nations. They do not make or worship
idols or images of their gods. They believe in
a supreme Creator (Katonda) whom however they do not
worship, as they consider him too exalted to pay any
attention to mankind. But they pay worship to inferior
gods or spirits, such as Mukusa, the god of the Lake
Nyanza, who at times enters into some person, man or
woman, who becomes his oracle and gains supernatural
powers. This personage consequently has great influence.
They also worship gods of war, Chiwuka and Neuda,
supposed to inhabit certain trees, before which, on going
to war, the Waganda offer live animals, which must be
black, and are given to the guardians of the trees. Various
natural forces, river gods, and the former kings are wor-

shipped as gods or demigods. Many superstitions are in vogue; and a multiplicity of charms are manufactured and sold by the "medicine-men," or mandwa, who profess to foretell events, cure diseases, bring rain and wind, and recover lost and stolen property.

The Waganda have a variety of games and amusements, including dancing, singing, and wrestling. The dancing in which the men and women keep separate, is of two kinds—one a sort of shuf- *Amusements.* fling, in which every muscle is writhing as in an epileptic fit, which is exceedingly exhausting; the other resembling European dancing. They have professional singers, accompanied on a sort of harp, and the singers often extemporise. There are regular bands of music, with leaders, the instruments being both stringed and wind, with drums.

The Uganda or Luganda language is called by Dr. Bleek a Bantu language, belonging to the great South African group. In these languages all inflex- *Language.* ions take place at the beginning of words. The Kiswahili of the East Coast is also understood by many of the people.

It seems difficult to realise that people can at the same time have so much good and so much bad in them. On the one hand, brave and warlike, on the other, *Contrasting* indolent; kindly to travellers, and even affec- *character-* tionate, and good servants, and at the same *istics.* time clever liars and thieves, and holding human life at a very low estimate; skilful in imitating articles of European manufacture, in learning a new language; allowing women to do nearly all their hard work; proficients at counting, the first thing they do with a book being to count the number of pages; having "all the vices and most of the diseases of Europeans," we must own that they possess much vitality and ability, having withstood so long their great losses in war and by the slave trade. But every one will hope that Uganda, with all its advantages, may yet become, as Mr. Wilson thinks it is well-fitted to be, the centre of light and civilization to the surrounding nations.

The Wanyoro are the next people to the north of the Waganda, but are a much less notable people. They are **The Wanyoro.** negroes, but not so dark, and include many light-brown people. Mr. Felkin gives a good account of their cleanliness and frequent ablutions, although their dome-shaped huts swarm with vermin. The people are great thieves and somewhat treacherous. Their dead are simply buried, without coffins, men on the left, the women on the right of the door of their huts. Clothing is not so extensively worn as by the Waganda. Skins clothe the men; girls are naked till marriage, and afterwards wear the bark-cloth. In many respects these people are an inferior copy of the Waganda.

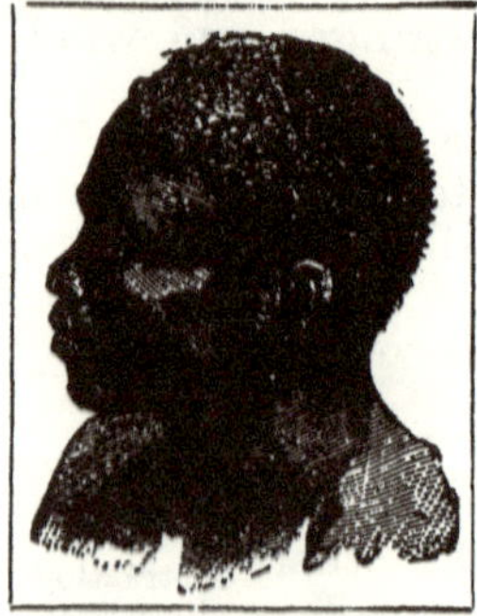

AKKA BOY.

Among them are some shepherd tribes called Longo, perhaps related to the Wahuma, leading independent lives and speaking a Galla dialect. The women are handsome, naked as to clothes, but loaded with ornaments of shell, girdles, bracelets, and rings. Their hair is elaborately dressed, every tress having variously coloured wool interwoven with it, and crowned with feathers, shell garlands, and imitations of buffalo horns.

To the north-west of Lake Albert Nyanza live the curious race of the Akka, of whom Dr. **The Akka.** Schweinfurth, when he was in the Monbuttu country, saw several, who were kept as a sort of court buffoons by the Monbuttu king. He also saw a band of several hundred of them upon one occasion. They are, as far as can be gathered (for Schweinfurth did not penetrate to their country), all of short stature, averaging about four feet ten inches in height, and some only reaching four feet one. But their peculiarities of physiognomy are more interesting even than their height. Their face, of a dull brown hue, has an extreme, almost monkey-like, forward projection of the jaws. In addition to thick lips, they have the upper jaw specially projecting under the nose, the line of which thus becomes very retreating. The skull is very round, almost spherical. Their eyes are large and wide-open, and their ears are very large. The sharply-defined, gaping mouth is a specially ape-like feature, in which they are unlike other negroes, but like the bushmen or Bosjesmen of South Africa. Their changes of expression, too, are very remark- *Peculiar* able. "The twitching of the eyebrows" (says *gestures.* Schweinfurth), "the rapid gestures with the hands and feet while talking, the incessant wagging and nodding of the head, all combine to give a very grotesque appearance to the little people." The arms are long and lanky, and the shoulders broad and peculiar in shape. Their hair and beard are but slightly developed, being brown, not black. They are specially a hunting people, showing much acuteness, dexterity, and cunning. They have only poultry as domestic animals. Several Akkas have been brought to Italy, and have thriven, learning to read and write with a facility which shows that they cannot be spoken of as a degenerate type. They are, rather, a small race which has been outstripped by people of larger make and greater physical force. Schweinfurth believes them to be, with the Bushmen, the Doko of the Upper Juba river, the Obongo, etc., the scattered remains of an aboriginal population now becoming extinct. Their language has not been ascertained, but their pronunciation seemed to Schweinfurth very inarticulate. Professor Flower, of the British Museum (Natural History), having measured two skeletons of Akkas, sent to England by Emin Pacha, concludes that they are the smallest known race, scarcely four feet high, and refers them to a special branch of the negroes, the Negrillos; differing in important respects from the Bushmen.

The Monbuttu inhabit a beautiful country, in which the Welle and other streams flowing to Lake Chad take their rise. They are a comparatively light- *The* coloured race, and noted for cannibalism. *Monbuttu.* When Schweinfurth visited them, they had a King Munza, who kept great state in a fine wooden *King Munza's* hall a hundred feet long, forty feet high, and *royal state.*

KING MUNZA IN FULL DRESS.

fifty broad. "A plumed hat rested on the top of his chignon, and soared a foot and a half above his head. This hat was a narrow cylinder of closely-plaited reeds; it was ornamented with three layers of red parrots' feathers, and crowned with a plume of the same; there was no brim, but a copper crescent projected from the front like the vizor of a Norman helmet. The cartilage of Munza's ears was pierced, and copper bars as thick as the finger inserted in the cavities." His whole body was smeared with a native unguent of powdered red cane-wood. His single garment was like that universally worn in the country, being a large piece of fig-bark dyed with the same unguent as his skin, and falling in folds about his body. Round thongs of buffalo-hide, with heavy copper balls attached to the ends, were fastened round the waist in a large knot, and held the "coat" like a girdle. Around his neck hung a copper ornament, and on his arms were pendent cylinders, bound with rings. Just below the knee were three circlets of hippopotamus hide, tipped

MONBUTTU WOMAN.

with copper. As a sign of authority Munza carried a sickle-shaped weapon of pure copper. His face was in some respects not very negro-like, telling of mixture with Hamitic and perhaps Semitic elements. His jaws were not protruding, but almost vertically under his forehead; but his lips were thick and prominent, a marked contrast to his straight Caucasian nose. His wives were dressed like other Monbuttu women, in notning but a pattern painted in black, showing up markedly upon their bright yellow skins. They wore huge chignons, and very few ornaments.

The Monbuttu are great cannibals, and Schweinfurth saw many skulls and portions of skeletons there, belonging to people south of them, captured in raids. Many had been undoubtedly boiled in. water and scraped with knives.

Cannibalism.

These people inhabit only a small extent of territory, but probably number a million. They do very little agriculture, or cattle breeding. Some of the men are good at smith's work; but except in war they are exceedingly idle, and women do most of the hard work—even making pottery. Food is carefully prepared, both human flesh and wild plantain and manioc. Oil from oil-palms is mixed with everything, as well as human fat.

Work and food.

Schweinfurth was astonished to find a large number of the Monbuttu with light hair, though it was still frizzled, and looked much like hemp. These were to a large extent Albinos, having light skins as well. In many ways they recall the Semitic type, and they differ from most negroes in having longer and curved noses. Schweinfurth's narrative gives many other interesting particulars which we cannot further dwell upon.

Albinos.

The Niam-Niam, living to the north of the Monbuttu, are another race of cannibals, their very name signifying "eaters"; they call themselves Zandey. They have round, broad heads, covered with thick frizzly hair of great length, arranged in long plaits and tufts. Their eyes are large, almond-shaped, and wide apart, in conformity with the width of the skull. The eyebrows are thick, and highly arched. The nose is very flat and broad, and the mouth is scarcely wider than the nostrils. The cheeks are full and rounded, giving a general circular aspect to the face. No one, according to Schweinfurth, could fail to identify the Niam-Niam at the first glance. The colour of their skin is a dull chocolate, and as marks of nationality they tattoo themselves with three or four squares of dots on foreheads, temples, or cheeks. On festivals they cover the body with powdered red wormwood, marked with a black

The Niam-Niam.

pattern in gardenia-juice. Their incisor teeth are filed to a point, to enable them to grip the arm of an enemy.

MONBUTTU WARRIORS.

Their height is an average one, and they are mostly rather fat.

Usually the Niam-Niam dress only in skins, fastened to a girdle round the loins. The men's hair is arranged in **Mode of hair-** a great variety of fashions, while the women's **dressing.** is scarcely dressed at all. In one style, the men have the hair drawn out into a series of rays, and stretched tightly over a hoop of considerable size, ornamented with cowries; and the hoop is fastened to the lower rim of a straw hat by four wires. The hat (worn only by men) is a cylindrical, brimless one, square at the top, which is decked with feathers; it is fastened by large and variegated hair-pins. Teeth arranged in various patterns, frequently including human teeth, are among their favourite ornaments.

Their weapons are chiefly lances and "trumbashes," sharp, flat projectiles of iron, with several pointed prongs **Weapons.** and sharp edges. They have large shields, with which they protect themselves from missiles. The Monbuttu supply them with most of their weapons. The men are mostly hunters, being very skilful in preparing traps and snares; while the women do all the agricultural work, eleusine, or "raffi," being the chief cereal. But the ground is exceedingly fertile, and natural fruits and other products most abundant. The **Meat-eating.** only domestic animals are poultry and dogs; and all kinds are eaten, besides many wild animals. Indeed, the propensity of the Niam-Niam to meat-eating is so great that the ordinary word for eating signifies **Cannibalism.** meat. All people conquered in war are eaten, as also are those who die friendless. Outside their houses are stakes on which are placed the skulls of those they have eaten; and human fat is universally sold. Altogether, the Niam-Niam are a very voracious people. There are, however, a certain proportion of them who loathe cannibals and cannibalism. Some have also attained the refinement implied in wiping the rim of a drinking vessel before passing it on. They drink and smoke largely. A kind of beer is made from malted eleusine; it has a pleasant bitter taste and a reddish-brown colour.

The Niam-Niam are not collected in towns, or even

considerable villages ; and their chiefs, of whom there are about thirty-five, have only a local authority. **Scattered dwellings.** Their huts, scattered over the country, are conical roofed, with clay walls. The roof projects outside the walls, and this part is supported by posts. Separate huts are used for cooking and sleeping. Some are elevated on clay bases, and have only one small opening above. These are for the boys to sleep in when they leave their mothers, and are supposed to be safe from wild beasts. Their granaries (of which there are usually three to each household) are raised upon posts; one of these stores serves to store malt for beer.

The Niam-Niam chiefs are called Beeáh, and their chief powers are those of calling the people to arms, executing those condemned to death, and determining questions of peace and war. **Chiefs.** They get the ivory and half the flesh of every elephant killed; but their chief support is derived from their farms, worked by slaves or wives. The chiefs rarely lead the people in person to battle, but wait its course at a distance, ready to decamp if defeat is declared. Battle has its interludes, occupied by hurling opprobrious epithets and shouts of defiance at one another. Schweinfurth says that the defiant imperiousness of some of the chiefs is equal to that of any potentate on earth. " The dread with which they inspire their subjects is incredible ; it is said that, for the purpose of exhibiting their power over life and death, they will occasionally feign fits of passion, and singling out a victim from the crowd, they will throw a rope about his neck, and with their own hands cut his throat with one stroke of their jagged scimitar." The eldest son of a chief succeeds to his position, the other sons command portions of his district, but often endeavour to set up independent authority, thus leading to wars.

Like most of their neighbours, the Niam-Niam know nothing of leather dressing, but make excellent earthenware, elaborate tobacco pipes, much carved and complex wood-work, and a variety of weapons. **Manufactures.** They have many instruments of music, and can stand music from morning to night. A kind of mandolin is

A NIAM-NIAM MINSTREL.

their favourite instrument, the strings being stretched vertically as in a harp, and there being a sound- Musical taste. ing board with two holes, a neck, and screws for tightening the strings. The music is very monotonous and unmelodious to European ears. There are professional musicians, too, who go about decked in fantastic costumes, and recite their adventures at great length for rings of copper, or beads.

Strange to say, wives are not bought by the Niam-Niam ; but application for wives is ordinarily made to the local chief or prince, who endeavours to Marriage. arrange a suitable match. There is unlimited polygamy, but there appears to be general fidelity ; indeed, the unfaithfulness of a wife is punished by death. Schweinfurth says that the men show a deep and consistent affection for their wives. The marriage ceremony is simply a procession of the bride to her new home, accompanied by musicians, minstrels, and jesters, followed by a feast. To the wives are assigned, besides preparing meals and cultivating the land, the important func-

NIAM-NIAM WOMAN.

tions of painting the husband's body and dressing his hair.

The Niam-Niam believe in evil spirits, who are supposed to dwell in the forest; they imagine that the rustling of the leaves is the talk of the spirits. They Beliefs. have various forms of augury and ordeal in regard to future events and suspected crime; but they cannot be said to have any form of idolatry. Language. Their language is akin to that of the Nubian or eastern Soudanese negroes; it has no separate tense for verbs, and many consonants, giving a nasal tone

even to the vowels " a " and " e." It is very deficient
in words denoting abstract ideas.

To the north-east of the Niam-Niam live the Bongo—
a people occupying the country around numerous affluents
of a large Nile tributary, the Ghazal. The country is
The Bongo. thinly peopled, and the Bongo are evidently
declining. They have been greatly coerced by
the Arab traders from Khartoum ; and their docility has
offered but too favourable opportunities for oppression and
slave-hunting. The Bongo are reddish-brown in complexion, notably like their soil. They are very round-
skulled (brachycephalic), like the Niam-Niam ; but their
hair is black, not much above half an inch long, and
whiskers and beards are scarcely ever to be seen.

The Bongo are naturally peaceful agriculturists, cultivating sorghum very carefully; they also rear poultry,
Habits. dogs, and goats, and do a good deal of hunting
and fishing.. Salt is not found in their country,
and they procure it by soaking the ashes of a shrub.
They are great tobacco growers and smokers, passing
their pipes from one to the other, as well as the lump
of bast to intercept the oil, and which the smoker puts
in his mouth. In great contrast to the Niam-Niam, the
Bongo abhor the eating both of human and of dog's flesh,
but they will eat all other flesh, even rats and snakes,
scorpions and caterpillars, and the " higher " the better.

Bongo men wear an apron of skin, or a piece of cloth
fastened to their girdle. The women wear neither, but
Dress. simply a branch with plenty of leaves, or a
bunch of fine grass. Their heads are often
closely shaven. The full-grown women become extremely
fat, their legs attaining the girth of a man's chest. To
make up for their lack of clothing, the women have a
great love of finery, wearing round their necks a quantity
Ornaments. of cords and beads, while the men wear necklaces adorned with bits of peculiar wood, roots,
owls' and eagles' talons, teeth of dogs, crocodiles, and
jackals, etc., and often adorn the rims of their ears with
copper rings. They also pierce the upper lip, and insert
a copper nail or plate, or rings. Even the skin of the

body above the waist is pinched up and pierced, a bit of wood being inserted, and iron rings of varied and elaborate pattern are worn over the wrist and forearm. The women also wear them on their ankles. The women's lower lip, after marriage, is pierced and extended by plugs of wood gradually increased in size, till it projects far beyond the upper, which is also bored, and a copper ring or plate is

HEAD-DRESS OF NIAM-NIAM.

inserted, or even a bit of straw. The sides of the nose are pierced for several bits of straw, and the septum for a large copper ring. The ears are perforated for rings in many places, and Schweinfurth says that there are women in the country whose bodies are pierced, in some way or other, in a hundred places. Tattooing is abundant on the upper part of the body of the women, in the shape of zigzag or parallel lines, or rows of dots.

Marriage is an affair of purchase, but it appears that a man is limited to three wives. The usual price for a **Marriage.** young girl is ten plates of iron, each weighing two pounds, and twenty lance-tips. Lack of children is an excuse for a divorce. The infants are carried on the mother's back in a bag of goat hide. The elder children of a family sleep in a hut by themselves.

Bongo huts are conical, with a circular seat on the top, from which the country around is viewed. The entrance **Dwellings.** to the huts is usually so small that it is necessary to creep through it on all-fours. The door is a hurdle swung on two posts. The floor is of clay carefully flattened. The people sleep on skins on the floor, with a stripped log of wood for a pillow. The usual corn store is under the dwelling, raised on posts as a protection against damp, rats, and white ants.

The Bongo are good smiths, much iron ore being found in their country. With the rudest apparatus **Smith work and smelting.** they make things not unworthy of an English smith. "Their smelting apparatus," according to Schweinfurth, "is an erection of clay, generally about five feet in height, containing in its interior three distinct compartments. These are all of the same size, that in the middle being filled with alternate layers of fuel and ore. This centre chamber is separated from the lower, by means of a kind of frame resting on a circular projection, and it is divided from the chamber above by a narrow neck of communication. The highest and lowest of the divisions are used for fuel only. Round the base of the inferior chamber there are four holes, into which the 'tewels' or pokers are introduced, and to which bellows are applied to increase the intensity of combustion; there is a fifth hole, which can be stopped with clay as often as may be desired, and which serves to allow the metal to be raked out after it has trickled down into the cavity below the frame."

The Bongo are sufficiently enterprising manufacturers to carry on a large trade with tribes lying to the north **Manufactures.** of them, and along the Upper Nile. Spades, spears, and axes are among the commonest productions, one very rough kind of circular spade being used as a medium of exchange, and thus answering to coin among the Bongo. Their chainwork, knives, pincers, etc., are quite remarkable, considering the simple apparatus at their disposal. Their woodwork is equally interesting. Their carved stools for women (the men refusing to sit on any raised seat), pestles, troughs, meshes, even figure-carvings to decorate a chief's grave, exhibit great skill and ingenuity. But Dr. Schweinfurth found that the influence of Mahometanism had caused much degeneration in these respects. "The destructive power of Islamism," he says, "has

Influence of Mahometans.

BONGO MAN.

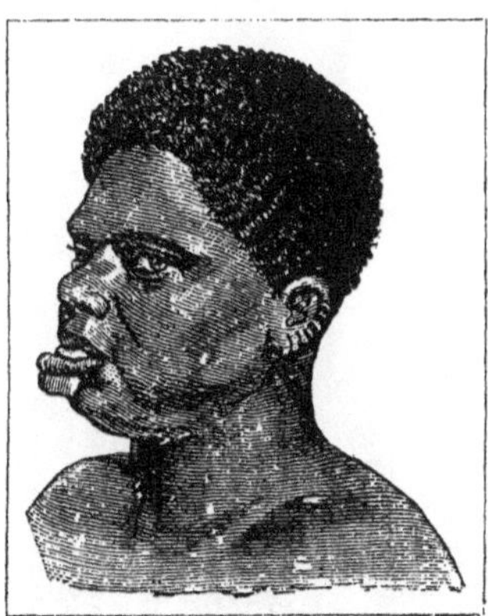

BONGO WOMAN.

manifested itself by obliterating, in a comparatively brief space of time, all signs of activity, and all traces of progress. Wherever it prevails, it annihilates the chief distinctions of race, it effaces the best vestiges of the past, and extends, as it were, a new desert upon the face of the land which it overruns." We must set this emphatic testimony of a scientific traveller as a counterpoise to much that has recently been asserted about the beneficial effects of Mahometanism.

These people make various kinds of musical instruments—flutes, monochords, drums, great trumpets, bones,

etc. At their great festivals the noise of the multitudinous instruments is described as "cats' music
run wild." Their singing too is extraordinary,
"it consists of a babbling recitative, which at one time suggests the yelping of a dog, and at another, the lowing of
a cow, whilst it is broken ever and again by the gabbling
of a string of words huddled up one into another. The
commencement of a measure will always be with a lively

Music and singing.

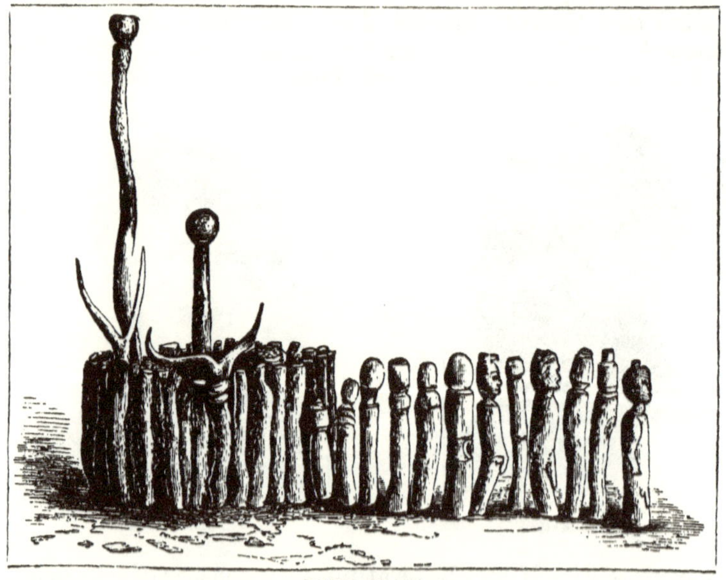

BONGO GRAVE.

air, and every one, without distinction of age or sex, will
begin yelling, screeching, and bellowing with all their
strength; gradually the singing of the voices will tone
down, the rapid tune will moderate, and the song is
hushed into a wailing, melancholy strain. Thus it sinks
into a very dirge, such as might be chanted at the grave,
and be interpreted as representative of a leaden and a
frowning sky, when all at once, without note of warning,
there bursts forth the whole fury of the negro throats."

Dr. Schweinfurth believes that these orgies are designed to imitate in their violence the fury of the elements.

The Bongo have no conception of a creator, or of any beneficial ruling power or spirit. They have a great fear of ghosts, which are believed to haunt every **Religious** place, and witches, generally old people, who **ideas.** consequently have a bad time of it. "Loma" denotes equally luck and ill-luck, and they use the same word for the "Allah," whom they hear the Mahometans call upon. They have no idea of immortality, or the transmigration **Burial.** of souls. They bury the dead immediately after death, the bodies being compressed into the smallest compass, and legs brought up to the chin, etc., and then sewn up in a sack made of skins. The grave is about four feet deep, and a side excavation is made at the bottom to receive the sack, so that there may be no pressure of the earth thrown in upon the body. The graves

BARI.

close to the huts are marked by long forked branches, carved with notches, and their points sharpened. The insane are bound hand and foot, and immersed **Treatment** in the river as a remedial measure; if this is **of the sick.** unsuccessful, they are confined and cared for by relatives. The sick are treated with very hot water sprinkled upon them; wounds have a number of setons passed through the wounded part, to reduce inflammation. Certain astringent bitter barks are about the only medicine they use. They sometimes employ professional magicians.

The Bongo language is of a usual negro type, with few words for abstract ideas, and is very simple in gram-

Language. mar. The words are harmonious in sound, abounding in the vowels *o* and *a*. The word "mony," originally denoting the grain sorghum, now signifies any kind of eatable, showing what they regard as "the staff of life."

Passing over some intermediate and smaller tribes, and again striking the Nile, we find the Bari negroes about

The Bari. Lado, and extending considerably to the north. Lado is well known as the scene of much of Dr. Emin's (Emin Bey) heroic efforts to govern and control the population, since the destruction of Egyptian influence in the Soudan. The Bari are fine-looking negroes of good bearing. The males wear no clothing, although a few fasten a string of beads round the waist, and a few bangles; a few ostrich feathers on their shaven heads complete the costume. The women are much more fully clad with rings, beads, chains, and shells, with a fringe in front, and a leather apron behind; but they, like the men, shave their heads. However, both sexes wear a gaudy coat of red paint, and tattoo themselves extensively.

Cattle are the great wealth of the Bari, who would rather lose wives or children than cows. The slave-

Value of dealers found this out, and used to capture the **cattle.** cattle first, and then exchange them for women and children. They are not killed for food, except for funeral feasts. They are bled, however, occasionally, and the blood used for food.

The Dinka, a pastoral people, occupy a large extent of country farther north. They are of good medium height,

The Dinka. perhaps slightly exceeding the average Englishman. They are among the darkest of races, and make themselves blacker with ashes. Their hair is very scanty, and generally closely shorn, except for a tuft at the top. In some cases the hair is specially trained to stand up all over the head, and dyed red, giving a very fiendish look. The beard is almost non-existent. There is the usual ear-piercing and lip-boring, which is so frequent that we shall only notice its absence or any special peculiarity.

According to these people, clothing is very unbecoming to men, and any man who is at all clothed is despised as a woman. Yet they wear rather extensive **Clothing and** head-dresses. The female sex is conspicuous **ornaments.** with aprons of skin behind and before, reaching to the ankles. Iron is the rage, copper not yet being of equal value; and the heavy rings with which the women load their wrists and ankles, says Schweinfurth, clink and resound like the fetters of slaves. Their ornaments and iron tools are chiefly the work of their neighbours, the Dyoor, unless they are sold to them by the traders from Khartoum. Their favourite weapons are however clubs and sticks, together with lances; they have also peculiar instruments for parrying club-blows.

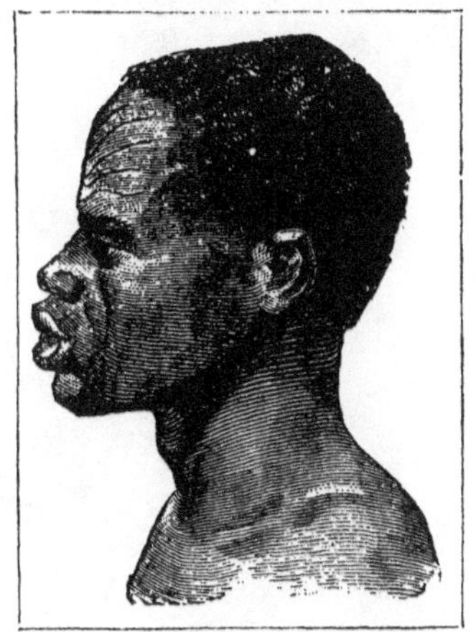

DINKA.

Unlike so many of their neighbours, the Dinka are both cleanly in person and in their cookery. They prepare and granulate their **Food.** meals in a very perfect way; they do not eat at the same time out of the same dish, but in succession. In the case of cooked meal, each pours his milk only on the portion he eats, and so a real measure of refinement is observed. As to animal food, the Dinka are very particular. Many of them would rather die of hunger than eat dog's flesh; but the hare and wild cat are among their dainties. Crocodile, frogs, lizards, mice, etc., they loathe; while they have a great regard for snakes, whose slaughter they look upon as a crime. Their dwellings **Dwellings.** are very clean, being large conical huts, some-times forty feet in diameter; in the middle, a tree trunk,

LLAMA CATTLE PARK.

with its spreading branches, supports the roof, made of layers of cut straw, supported at the edges in branches of acacia and other hard woods.

Oxen, sheep, goats, and dogs are plentiful, but poultry are never seen. The cattle are zebu-like, with humps, and mostly white. The Dinka vocabulary for **Regard for** cattle-breeding is remarkably copious, and they **animals.** show them the greatest regard, never killing them. The proprietor will not even eat his dead cow, though his neighbours will readily enough. All their animals are of degenerate breeds, and give little milk, poor in butter. Their animals are kept in great parks, and tethered to pegs at night. So numerous are the cattle, that there are probably three for every human being.

Although cattle-breeders, the Dinka are sufficiently warlike to be formidable, and their independence has not been broken through. They are unrelenting to enemies, though very kind to each other.

The Shillooks inhabit the left, or western bank of the White Nile, for two hundred miles, occupying a district of ten miles wide, as far as the Bahr-el-ghazal, **The Shillooks.** or Gazelle river. They are densely packed all along the river; agriculture, fishing, cattle-breeding, hunting, are all easy and profitable; and thus the Shillooks supply a constant stream of emigrants, pushing in a south-westerly direction. They are very dark negroes, made more repulsive by the constant plastering of the body with ashes, by their lean boniness of limb, and their breaking off of the lower central incisors. "The move-ments of their lean bony limbs are so languid," says Schweinfurth, " and their repose so perfect, as not rarely to give the Shillooks the resemblance of mummies; and whoever comes as a novice amongst them can hardly resist the impression that in gazing at those ash-grey forms, he is looking upon mouldering corpses, rather than upon living beings." Yet their skulls indicate a rather high level of the negro type, with narrower jaws and less prominent noses.

These people devote much attention to their hair, the men plucking out the beard, but plastering the head with

clay, gum, or dung, and arranging the hair like a comb,
Hair dressing. helmet, or fan.   The women have short cropped hair.   In many other respects, however, their habits are like those of the Dinkas.   They appear to have
Religious ideas. no very complex religious ideas, but reverence an imagined Father of their people, who brought them to their country.   When famine comes, or rain is wanted, they call upon him by name.   They suppose that the dead still linger among the living.

Darfur is the most westerly territory into which the late Egyptian dominion extended.   On the west is the

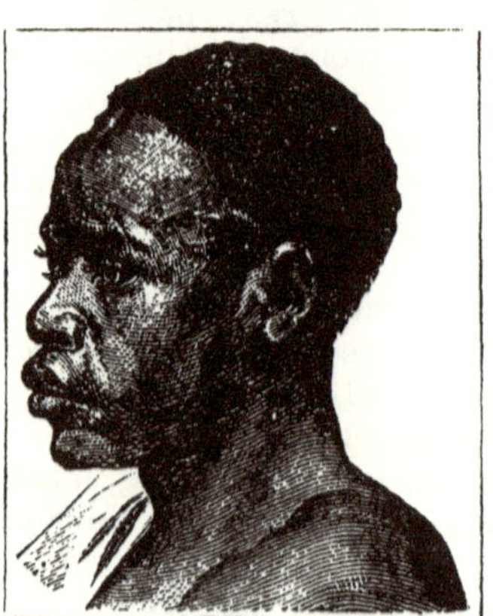

FUR.

Darfur. kingdom of the Wadaï; on the north, the south-eastern Sahara and the Libyan desert. The word means the land of the Furs or Fors, a negro people now largely driven by the Arabs into the western tracts. But all profess Mahometanism. The country, previous to the Egyptian annexation, had been under a line of absolute rulers or sultans, for at least four hundred years. Its conquest by Zebehr Pasha in 1874, with the death of the sultan Brahim, is well known; but Zebehr was too much a "king of the slave-dealers," and too grasping, and his subsequent downfall and expulsion from Egypt were fully justified.   What the present government of Darfur is, it would be difficult to say.

According to Mr. Felkin the natives (Fors) are great hunters, and clean and industrious.   The children clean
The Fors. and spin cotton, which the men weave into a cloth of which their clothing is made.   The women not only attend to the household, but also cultivate the ground and weave mats.   The men wear long shirts with wide sleeves; the women a large sheet bound

round the waist, and one corner thrown over the left
shoulder ; their arms and necks being adorned with iron
and brass ornaments. The people are very hospitable,
and but for the Arab slave-hunts, which keep them in
continual fear, would live in comfort. In some parts
there are large numbers of camels and hump-backed
cattle. Camel-hair cloth is made in the camel districts.
Their horses are very fine, though small, and can do any
amount of work.

Kordofan, the country between Darfur and the White
Nile, extending almost to Khartoum, is largely desert-
like, and its population is but a few hundred **Kordofan.**
thousands. Little is cultivated except the
penicillaria or dokn, which is the staple food. Gum,
hides, and ostrich feathers are the chief exports. Water
is scanty, and is stored in the large hollow trunks of the
baobab tree, often thirty or forty feet round, and capable
of containing twenty thousand gallons. Here the late
Mahdi's power centred ; but it is doubtful if he has left
any permanent impress on the people. Near Obeid, the
capital, a red brick city of 3,500 people, the **Mixture of**
population is dense and very mixed, including **people.**
Arabs, Nubians, Egyptians, and various negroes. Mr.
Felkin describes them as above the average height,
rather slender in figure, with well-shaped heads and dark
brown skins. Their oval faces and straight noses, and
well-formed chins give them a decidedly handsome appearance. About ten years old, girls begin to wear a little
girdle ; men only wear one piece of cloth and sandals,
and shave the head with the exception of a pigtail ;
women are almost as little covered, but plait their hair
in long locks, arranged like a thatched roof. The women
also wear ivory and silver arm and ankle rings, earrings,
nose-rings, etc., and nearly every one has numerous
charms, from traffic in which the Mahometan fakirs drive
a good trade.

The marriage arrangements are curious in Kordofan.
Marriage. Before a girl marries, says Mr. Felkin, a con-
tract is made as to how many free nights a week
she shall have, the usual agreement being that every

fourth night shall be at her own disposal. In one section of the people, no girl is allowed to marry until she has borne a child, which she must give to her brother to be his slave. Among others, a girl's husband is chosen at a young men's flogging match, held in presence of the elder people and of the girl. The youth who can stand the most stripes is the husband selected. If two men claim a girl, she may sit between them, having a knife securely fixed to each forearm, and projecting behind the elbow, and slowly pierce their thighs with it. Three village elders sit by and judge which of the would-be husbands endures this ordeal with most fortitude, and he is the chosen bridegroom.

It is not surprising to learn that the moral character of the people is bad. "Murder is very common, thieving **Morals.** is an ordinary occupation, they are untruthful, lazy, and unchaste, and can never be induced to work more than is absolutely necessary for bare existence. They never go about unarmed, and seem capable of making very little progress towards civilization." Mahometanism does not seem to have done them much good.

The Nubas. The Nubas of Kordofan are the origin of the Nubians proper, but are now feebler and fewer than their relatives. They are largely driven into the mountains, hunted by slave-dealers. They dress like Arabs, but are very distinguishable by their dark skins and prominent jaws. They are not very intelligent, but are honest as far as they go. Among the Arabs they profess Mahometanism, but among themselves they retain their witch-doctors and rain-makers. Their dialect differs considerably from that of the Nubians.

The Dogola or Dogolowis live in mountains of that name, near the Nubas, but their language and gestures **Dogolowis.** are very different. Their jaws are not so prominent. Their features are more regular, and their nose is not so flat. They are much more intelligent than the Nubas. They have a very independent spirit, and resisted the Egyptians valiantly. They are very skilful smiths, and import iron to make their own weapons and implements.

A number of nomad tribes,—divided into Kababish, or camel and goat-herds, and Baggara, or cattle-herds,— occupy the desert and less settled parts of Kordofan. The Baggara call themselves Arabs, and speak Arabic with a peculiar pronunciation. They are elephant-hunters as well as cattle-keepers. Their skin is reddish, like the American Indians, and their form is athletic and elegant. The women wear still an ancient Egyptian sort of head-dress. They were among the most zealous of the Mahdi's followers. *Kababish and Baggaras.*

The mountains of Senaar, the " Mesopotamia of the two Niles," are the home of the tribes known as Funj, formerly much more widely spread. They maintained a kingdom of Senaar till the beginning of the present century; but Mahomet Ali conquered them in 1821. They have now lost their old language, and in adopting Mahometanism many of them are greatly mingled with Arabs and other races; and it is said that people of all colours—white, red, yellow, blue, green, and black—are to be met with in Senaar. The Funj are of a type intermediate between Nubians, negroes proper, and Gallas. They have long heads, vertical jaws, regular features, and good figures; and they are pleasant and hospitable. The women are said to keep their youthful appearance a long time—a rare thing in Africa. Friction of the body, fumigation with aromatics and anointing with fat, are much in vogue among them. Senaar people are even noted as skilful surgeons. *The Funj.*

The junction of the two Niles is the seat of the populous town of Khartoum, long an important place, where Turks, Egyptians, Arabs, Nubians, negroes, and Gallas met and trafficked. Soldiers, merchants, and slaves crowded its streets; grain, cotton, gums, ivory ebony, and ostrich feathers were exchanged for European goods. It has very considerably the appearance of an Egyptian city, with its minarets and mosques and whitewashed houses. Its disorganised and degenerate state since the calamitous fate of Gordon, contrasted with its improvement when under his control, is proof of the great loss the Soudan experienced when he was killed. *Khartoum.*

CHAPTER VI.
The Central Soudanese.

African empires—The kingdom of Bornu—Mahomet El-Kanemi—Kuka—
Difficulties of barter—The Bornuese or Kanuri—Slavery—Government—
Signs of distinction — The Shuwa Arabs — The Marghi — Adamawa —
Baghirmi—Description of people—Currency—Negroes of Southern Bag-
hirmi—Marriage customs—Religion—Kingdom of Wadai—The Mabas—
Government of Wadai—Fulahs or Fellatahs—Gando and Sokoto — Barth's
description of Kano—The Haussas—Feudalism—Moassina—Former Song-
hay kingdom—Timbuktu.

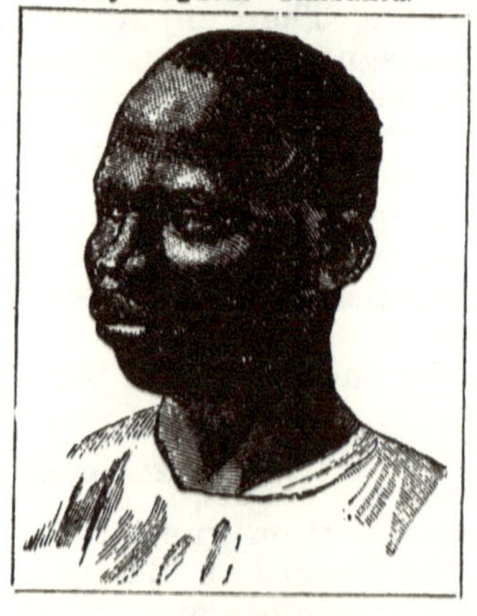

KANURI.

THE vast and thickly-peopled domains of the central Soudanese rulers have been largely made known to us in modern times by the celebrated German travellers Barth, Rohlfs, and Nachtigal. By their accounts of Bornu, Baghirmi, and Wadai, and of the Fulah empires further west, they have done much to transform our ideas as to the powers of organisation, and even of civilisation, of the negro races. They have shown us that far from Europe and Asia, with its various Aryan, Semitic, and Mongoloid types of civilisation, exhausting the possibilities of civil polity, there is a complex attempt at government, and even a kind of culture, in Africa, of which we had little conception.

106

Approaching Bornu and Lake Chad from the Sahara, a striking change comes over the scene. The country becomes as fertile and prolific as it was previously barren. Mimosa forests and grassy tracts occupy the border-lands. The hippopotamus and crocodile are to be found in the lake, and an archipelago in it is inhabited by the Yedina, or race of negro pirates, independent of Bornu.

The kingdom of Bornu has annals dating back at least to the middle of the sixteenth century, and purporting to go back to the seventh or ninth centuries. **The kingdom** Mahometanism has been established there for **of Bornu.** eight hundred years, and a succession of dynasties have held absolute power. At the beginning of this century the kingdom began to be harassed by the Fulbe or Fellatah, who had conquered the Haussa territories, and now destroyed the capital of Bornu. A fakir, **Mahomet** Mahomet El-Kanemi, saved the country, how- **El-Kanemi.** ever, and founded a new capital, securing for himself substantial power under the title of sheikh, while the nearest heir of the former rulers was installed as sultan. El-Kanemi ruled, at the new city of Kuka, with great severity, and obtained a great reputation for sanctity, partly by punishing trivial things (such as women walking out unveiled or talking too loudly) most severely. His son, Sheikh Omar, succeeded to power in 1835, and deposed the nominal sultan. It does not appear that the promise of a strong power being maintained in Bornu is being fulfilled, although its commercial importance is very great.

Kuka, the present capital, is a crowded market for all sorts of African produce. Strangely enough, it is in two separate parts, large oblongs, separated by **Kuka.** nearly a mile, in one of which (the eastern) the sultan with his troops and slaves resides. The houses are of the conical African form, of reeds and straw; some few, however, being built of clay. It is the slave-trade on which the prosperity of Bornu is based, although a multiplicity of other merchandise is here disposed of.

A slight specimen of the mode of doing business at Kuka will show that marketing has its difficulties. Barth

says that a great many difficulties arise from the absence
Difficulties of of a common standard of value among the
barter. various people who resort to the market. " A
small farmer who brings his corn to the Monday market,

will on no account take his payment in shells, and will
rarely accept of a dollar. The person therefore who
wishes to buy corn, if he has only dollars, must first
exchange a dollar for shells, or rather buy shells; then

with the shells he must buy a shirt; and after a good deal of bartering, he may thus succeed in buying the corn." The fatigue to be undergone in the market is such that Barth's servants very often returned in the utmost exhaustion; but most things can be obtained very cheaply. Camels sell at from eight to twenty dollars.

Although a great mixture of people may be encountered in Bornu, the bulk of the inhabitants are a mixed negro race, known as Bornuese, or Kanuri, with high **The Bornuese** foreheads, broad noses, thick lips, and large **or Kanuri.** mouths. The women are the worse looking, having short, square figures, and very large nostrils, disfigured by a red bead or piece of coral stuck in the left side. The usual dress is one or more indigo blue skirts, the better class wearing a blue cap, while the sultan and his officials wear the red fez. The women wear their hair in several thick rolls, one over each ear, and another over the middle of the head, the three being united on the forehead. They are extensively tattooed, and stain their faces with indigo. Their incisor teeth are dyed black, and their canine teeth red, giving them a horrible appearance. Polygamy prevails, and the marriage ceremonies— which are complex, and which include much feasting— last a week.

Mahometanism is the State religion of Bornu, and is held with fanaticism by its devotees. Thus all who do not practise it are liable to be carried off and **Slavery.** sold as slaves. Notwithstanding this, many of the people subject to Bornu retain Paganism. The sultan or sheikh is a despotic ruler, though observing numerous forms of constitutionalism. The number of tributary peoples and rulers is so considerable as to give **Government.** rise to a comparison with European feudalism; each chief has his own body of soldiers, and the total military force is very considerable, many of the soldiers being armed with guns. The sultan's bodyguard is a troop of horsemen clad in armour, partly manufactured in Bornu. He even possesses a number of cannon cast in Kuka.

One feature very essential to a chief is to have a

large " corporation," and if he is unable to secure this by
Signs of distinction. luxurious feeding, he pads up to the required
dimensions.   Another sign adopted to show
distinction is to wear as many garments as possible.   A
large number of turbans are also worn.

Among the Bornuese, as in other kingdoms around, are
many encampments of Arab tribes, who are known as

KANURI WOMAN, BORNU.

Shuwa Arabs. S h u w a,
some having fixed villages.
Although long resident in Bornu, they
preserve their race
type very completely,
being middle-sized,
rather slender, with
dark olive complexions, and generally
pleasing features.
Their Arabic language, however, is
rather degenerate, for
a Shuwa is not able
to say three words
without inserting his
favourite " kuch,
kuch," which signifies
"thorough," or "berkelek," " your worship."

The Marghi tribe,
south of Bornu, are
heathen negroes, who
go entirely naked except for a strip of leather, and are
The Marghi. unusually good-looking for negroes.   Their
faces are not disfigured by incisions, and their
complexion varies from black to light yellow.   Both sexes
are tall, and the women, especially when red-coloured, become repulsive with their long, hanging breasts, and the
metal plates worn in their under lips.   One of their pecu-

liar customs is to mourn for the death of a young man, and make merry at the death of an old one.

The large province of Adamawa, south of Bornu, is another stronghold of Mahometanism, established by a Fulah, Fulbe, or Pullo chief, Adama, by the overthrow of the former Pagan kingdom of **Adamawa.** Fumbina. The Fulahs have largely immigrated into it, have occupied many of the best positions, and in some parts extirpated or driven out the natives. It is one of the finest countries of Central Africa, being well irrigated by tributaries of the Chadda or Benué, the great affluent of the Niger. Among the negro tribes of the country, the Batta, the Fali, the Mbum, etc., are important.

The kingdom of Bornu now extends round the greater part of the circumference of Lake Chad, except at the south-east, where the kingdom of Baghirmi **Baghirmi.** has a share of the lake coast. Baghirmi, in its turn, was reduced in 1871 by the Sultan Ali of Wadai but a short account of Baghirmi may be given separately. Mahometanism entered it some time later than Wadai. The country is well watered by the Shari, and its tributaries, flowing to Lake Chad, and is very fertile, growing millet and other grains (not wheat), rice growing wild.

The Baghirmi people are for the most part better looking than those of Bornu,—the men being bigger, stronger, and more courageous; while the women are **Description** also taller and well-proportioned, with regular **of people.** features and a pleasing expression. Their nostrils are not nearly so broad as those of Bornu women. They bestow considerable care upon their hair, raising it like the crest of a helmet. Their dress is simply a black mantle fastened across the breast.

The currency in Baghirmi consists chiefly of strips of cotton; large articles are bought with shirts. Shells are not currency, but are bought as articles of **Currency.** merchandise to export into Pagan countries. The people have made considerable progress in dyeing and weaving. Their chief weapon is the spear; there are very few shields or coats of mail.

In the southern parts of Baghirmi Pagan tribes are

CENTRAL AFRICAN HOUSES, WEAPONS, IMPLEMENTS, ETC.

A.—1. Shield of buffalo hide. 2. Helmet of negroes' hair, with cowry shells and ostrich feathers. 3. Dwelling of clay and grass. 4. Bow for parrying blows with clubs. 5. Water-jug of clay. 6. Iron lance-point. 7. Big drum for beating the alarm. 8. Iron lance of one piece, a weapon of parade.

B.—1. Axe for splitting wood. 2. Horn spoon. 3. Bellows, made of two vessels of clay opening into a third. 4. Arm ornaments, made of iron rings. 5. Tattooing on women's arms. 6. Comb of bamboo. 7. Fire-striking apparatus of anona-wood. 8. Iron lance-point with hook.

C.—1. Tobacco pipe of clay. 2. Pipe of ceremony, with wooden stem and clay bowl. 3. Hurling-irons. 4. Inner side of a wooden shield. 5. Stool and dining-table out of one block. 6. Bedstead of thick stems stripped of the bark. 7. Corn magazine with movable roof.

D.—1. Sickle-formed, iron, double-edged cutting weapon; the handle of wood wound round with iron. 2. Iron hatchet, with wooden handle. 3. Bow, with guard for the arm. 4. Quiver of plaited reed, with arrows. 5. Palace hut of palm-trunks, grass, and banana-leaves.

still in the ascendant. They are mostly allied to the Songhay, a race whose empire formerly stretched north as far as Morocco. They are short and unpleasing in looks, and their dress is merely a narrow band of skin round the loins. Their hair is dressed most elaborately. Both sexes have one incisor knocked out. They have many horses, which they manage well, without saddle or stirrups. Their weapons are chiefly spears and knives, and they protect themselves with shields of buffalo hide. *Negroes of Southern Baghirmi.*

These people are industrious agriculturists, growing millet and durra, which they exchange for tobacco, cowry shells, and pearls. They live in straw houses, but store their corn in conical mud huts. They are also considerably pastoral, having horses, sheep, goats, and dogs, the latter being much liked for eating. Neither cats nor oxen are found among them.

They have a very peculiar marriage custom. A childless wife may be sold as a slave; but when three children have been born, the wife may, if she chooses, go back to her parents, as the husband may then be supposed to have received an equivalent for his marriage payment. The dead are buried in circular graves, in which various provisions for the deceased are also placed, and cowry shells as money. Some tribes are said to bury a boy and a girl alive with a deceased person, ostensibly to keep off flies. *Marriage customs.*

These negroes believe in a supreme being, whose voice is heard in the thunder, and whose symbol is a tree trunk, with the bark removed in rings, set up near their houses in a little sanctuary, from which women and children are excluded. Naturally witchcraft and sorcery are believed in by this people, who make elaborate inquiries for its detection. *Religion.*

East of Baghirmi and Lake Chad, extending north and east as far as Darfur, and bordering on the Niam-niam in the south, is the large kingdom of Wadai. It derived its Mahometanism from the east, from Arab invaders. It is on the whole flat, with numerous dry and sterile tracts, interspersed with many streams, *Kingdom of Wadai.*

which only in the wet season reach Lake Chad. It also includes the upper Shari basin. It is peopled by a heterogeneous mixture of tribes—Arab, Negroes, Fulahs, etc.

The Mabas. The Negroes include the Mabas, the most numerous people, and although they are Mahometans, Arabs do not appear to be in high favour; up to a recent period they could not venture into Abeshr, the capital. The people are much below those of Bornu in all social qualities, although some of the negro tribes have vigorous bodily frames and great courage. Few of their towns or villages are of any great extent; and, as usual in Central Africa, the houses are bell-shaped and built of reed, except in the case of the sultan and some of his principal officers and chiefs, which are built of clay. The Arabs, however, use portable huts of mats made of palm leaves. There are no considerable markets; barter is much in vogue, and trade is largely carried on by travelling merchants from the Nile valley. The chief traffic is in slaves, ivory, and ostrich feathers.

In character the natives of Wadai are violent, quarrelsome, and cruel, and very much given to drinking durra beer. They have also a great antagonism to all foreigners, which has very largely prevented the country from being accessible. Both meat and grain are plentiful, cattle, sheep, and goats being very numerous; dokn (penisetum) is the chief grain, being ground between stones instead of in the large wooden mortar so much used in Central Africa. They have quite a large variety of dishes, and undoubtedly fare well on the whole.

The Sultan (Ali) of Wadai is a powerful and despotic ruler, supported by fanatical Mahometans learned in the **Government** Koran. The government is very vigorous, deal-**of Wadai.** ing greatly in death sentences, and in cutting off noses and ears; it puts down cheating of all kinds relentlessly. The sultan's tribute is exacted by various local governors or agents.

South of Wadai are numerous tribes not yet much known, and termed Banda tribes; some of whom are cannibals.

Passing now to the westward, and approaching the

Niger, we come to the domains conquered by the Mahometan Fulahs, or Fellatahs, who, becoming con- The Fulahs verted in the middle of the eighteenth century, or Fellatahs. carried a warlike propagandism through the Western Soudan, and succeeded in establishing their supremacy very widely. Some term them the most intelligent of all the African tribes. They are of a much lighter complexion than the true negroes, often being ruddy-coloured.

WEDDING CEREMONY, EQUATORIAL AFRICA.

Many are tall and slender, and have regular features, long black hair, not frizzled, and are by some thought to be a distinctly Caucasian type; others, probably on the best grounds, identify them with the Hamites. Undoubtedly they present varying characters in different localities, from their having intermixed with various peoples. Thus we might perhaps best regard them as a new type evolved in recent times, and including the most intelligent and active people to be found in Central and Western Soudan. Their language has most affinities with negro types.

It was only in 1802 that the Sheikh Othman, a religious enthusiast, living under the ruler of Gober, a northern *Gando and* district of Sokoto, raised the standard of re- *Sokoto.* volt, and after being often defeated, established a large empire at Gando. His son, Mohammed Bello, received the eastern portion of the dominion, Sokoto; while his brother, Abd-Allahi, gained the northern part, known as Gando.

The Fulahs are certainly not so numerous as the negro people among whom they live and whom they rule. They live *Barth's* in large towns, some *description* of which are great *of Kano.* centres of commerce, protected by good walls of mud and dry moats. Kano, one of the chief of these, deserves some description, derived from Barth's graphic narrative : " It includes a great variety of clay houses, huts, sheds, green open places affording pasture, deep hollows containing ponds, beautiful trees and plants, the papau, the date palm, the silk cotton tree ; people, in all varieties of cos-

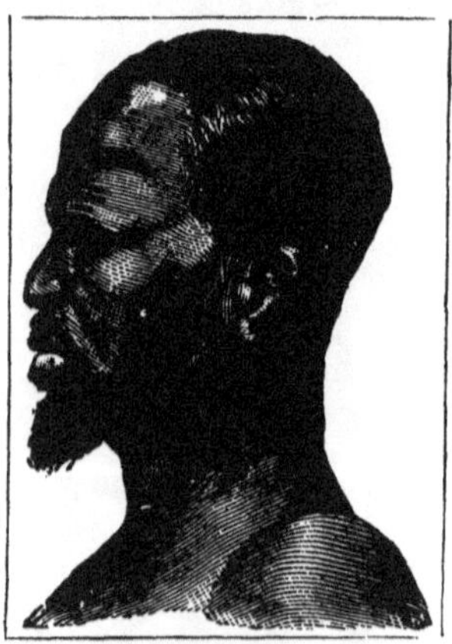

HAUSSA.

tume, from the naked slave to the most gaudily dressed Arab. Here a row of shops, filled with articles of native and foreign produce, with buyers and sellers in every variety of figure, complexion, and dress, yet all intent upon their little gain, endeavouring to cheat each other; there a large shed, like a hurdle, full of half-naked, half-starved slaves, anxiously watching into whose hands it should be their destiny to fall. In another part were to be seen all the necessaries of life; the wealthy buy- ing the most palatable things for his table ; the poor stopping and looking greedily upon a handful of grain; here a rich governor, dressed in silk and gaudy clothes, mounted upon a spirited and richly caparisoned horse, and followed by a host of idle, insolent slaves; there a poor blind man groping his way through the multitude, and fearing at every step to be trodden down; here a yard neatly fenced with mats of reed, and provided with all the comforts which the country affords—a clean, snug-looking cottage, the clay walls nicely polished, a shutter of reeds placed against the low, well-rounded door, a cool shed for the daily household work—a fine spreading tree affording a pleasant shade during the hottest hours of the day; the matron in a clean black cotton gown, wound round her waist, her hair neatly dressed in chokoli or bejaji, busy preparing the meal for her absent husband, or spinning cotton, and at the same time urging the female slaves to pound the corn; the children, naked and merry, playing about in the sand; earthenware pots and wooden bowls, all cleanly washed and standing in order. . . . Now a busy marina, an open terrace of clay, with a number of dyeing pots, and people busily employed in various processes of the handicraft; here a man stirring the juice, and mixing with the indigo some

FULB (FELLATA).

colouring wood in order to give it the desired tint; there another, drawing a shirt from the dye-pot, or hanging it up on a rope fastened to the trees; there two men beating a well-dyed shirt, singing the while, and keeping good time; further on, a blacksmith busy with his rude tools in making a dagger (which will surprise by the sharpness of its blade those who feel disposed to laugh at the workman's instruments), a formidable barbed spear, or the more estimable and useful implements of husbandry; in another place, men and women making use of an ill-frequented thoroughfare to hang up along the fences their

cotton thread for weaving; close by, a group of indolent
loiterers, lying in the sun and idling away their hours.
Here a caravan from Gonja arriving with the desired
kola-nut, chased by all who have ten kurdi to spare from
their necessary wants, or a caravan laden with natron,
starting for Nupe, or a troop of Asbenawa going off with
their salt for the neighbouring towns, or some Arabs,
leading their camels, heavily laden with the luxuries of
the north and east, to the quarter of the Ghadamsiye;
there a troop of gaudy, warlike-looking horsemen, gallop-

WOMAN OF MASSINA. WOMAN OF SONINKE. KHASSONKE GIRL.

ing towards the palace of the governor to bring him the
news of a new inroad of Serki Ibram. Everywhere
human life in its varied forms, the most cheerful and the
most gloomy, seemed closely mixed together; every
variety of national form and complexion: the olive-
coloured Arab; the dark Kanuri, with his wide nostrils;
the small-featured, light and slender Ba-Fellanchi; the
broad-faced Mandingo; the stout, large-boned and mascu-
line-looking Nupe female, the well-proportioned and
comely Ba-Hanshe woman."

The Haussa negroes form the mass of the population, and have long adopted Mahometanism. They are said, by those who know them well, to be distin- The Haussas. guished for their vivacity, intelligence, friendli- ness, industry, and social qualities. The Haussa tongue is described as the noblest, the most harmonious, the richest, and the most animated in all negroland, and it is understood very widely in Central Africa.

It would be fruitless to attempt to describe the many loosely-knit States that make up the large empire of Sokoto. The Fulah sultan has something like Feudalism. a feudal system under him, and the governors of some of the chief provinces are hereditary tributaries.

Gando, east of Sokoto, is still less definite than Sokoto, and has recently come under British protection. It in- cludes the territory of the Nupe negroes, with numerous large towns, and the seat of a native African bishop of the English Church.

Moassina, or Massina, occupying both sides of the Niger from Bambarra to Kabara, the port of Timbuktu, is also a considerable kingdom; and its chief town, Moassina. Jenne, does a large trade in salt and gold. In this kingdom are to be found scattered remnants of the Sonrhays, or Songhays, a people formerly dominant in Western Africa, but now distinguished for inhospitality and sullenness, wearing nothing but leather aprons where they are independent, but adopting the indigo dyed shirt where the Fulahs have the upper hand.

The Songhay kings embraced Mahometanism in the eleventh century, A.D., and had received their civilisation from Egypt. About 1488 they conquered Timbuktu from Former the Tuareg, and laid the foundation of its Songhay importance by inducing the rich caravan mer- kingdom. chants from the north to settle there, and make it the great emporium of trade between Western and Northern Africa. It is probable these kings afford us the highest example of sovereign capabilities in the negro race. Their conquests were extended from 12° north to the south of Morocco, and from the centre of the Haussa states to the borders of the Atlantic, and it is testified of them that they governed their subjects with justice, and greatly improved their well-being and comfort.

Timbuktu itself never played more than a secondary part, except in trade; and its importance is not in its productions, but in its being a convenient market at the convergence of several routes. It was formerly much larger than it is now. It is unwalled, with about a thousand clay houses, and a couple of hundred conical huts of matting: there are three large mosques. Salt and gold are the chief articles of traffic, cloth manufactured in Kano being very much employed as a means of barter. The kola nut is also an important article of merchandise.

CHAPTER VII.
The Western Africans, from the Senegal to the Ogoway.

The French in Senegambia—The Joloffs and Mandingoes—Cape Verd Islanders—British settlements—Sierra Leone—Liberia—The Kru-men—The Gold Coast—The Fantis—Dress and ornaments—Moral character—Government—Fetishism—Burial—The Ashantis—The king's palace—Houses—Treasures and grandeur—Government—Human victims—Punishment of crime—The Ffons of Dahomey—The Amazons—Mode of fighting—The Customs—Fetishism—The Yorubas and Egbas—Physical characters—Mode of salute—Superstitions—The Oil Coast—Cruel practices—Mumbo Jumbo—The people `Abo—Marriage—A slave market—The Cameroons—The Gaboon country—French possessions.

JOLOFF.

THE native negro races enjoy almost a monopoly of this great tract of country, owing to its unhealthiness for Europeans, and even for negroes who have been born in more temperate climes. The French have settled at St. Louis, Dakar (Cape Verd), and Goree, and since 1854, when General Faidherbe became governor, have gained control of the southern bank of the Senegal river and the adjacent territory, and the coast nearly

The French in Senegambia.

to the river Gambia, as well as some isolated settlements south of this towards Sierra Leone. They are moreover establishing a connection, across the Sahara, with their Algerian possessions, and have brought under their control

WOMEN OF SENEGAMBIA.

the King of Sego, on the Niger, who rules over the Bambarras, a branch of the Mandingoes.

A good part of the maritime and plain country between the Senegal and the Gambia is inhabited by the Joloffs, who have a dark, grey-bronze complexion, with little hair, and very prominent jaws and under-lips. They **The Joloffs** are remarkable for the number of amulets, **and** rings, coins, etc., they wear on neck, hands, **Mandingoes.** and legs. Further up the hills the Mandingoes and Bambarras prevail, occupying the large territory known as Futa-Jallon, from which most of the tribes of this coast take their rise. Into this have penetrated large numbers of Fulahs, or Fellatahs. Fokumba has been made a holy

city by the Mahometans; Timbo is the principal town. The Mandingoes are a fine negro type,—being tall, with long, frizzly hair, and of very dark complexion. Probably they number in all six to eight millions. To a large extent they are outwardly Mahometans.

MANDINGO TRADER.

We may here break off to mention the Cape Verd Islands, about 350 miles west of Cape Verd, and belonging **Cape Verd** to Portugal. The **Islanders.** population includes a number of pure negroes, but the majority are European and African half-breeds, mostly ignorant and uncleanly. They all profess Roman Catholicism, but retain many heathenish practices and superstitions. Agriculture is industriously carried on, together with weaving, and oil and sugar refining. But the entire population does not reach one hundred thousand.

From the Gambia to the Liberian republic the British settlements are numerous, and their influence extends over a wide tract of the interior. Bathurst, **British** Sierra Leone, Sherboro' Island are among the **settlements.** chief settlements, having fine houses for the very few

Europeans, and a crowded population of half-clad negroes,
Mandingoes, Joloffs, etc., who live in simple huts of bam-
boos and palm leaves. Sierra Leone has gone through
many vicissitudes since its settlement in 1787. It was
long the seat of the disastrous efforts to build up a com-
Sierra Leone. munity of the slaves captured from slave-traders,
and set free by our naval forces; and their
descendants form the bulk of the population, and act as
though they were the lords of creation. For a time the
government was very largely given into their hands, and
they took advantage of it to bring in verdicts invariably
against whites and in favour of themselves, and to display
feelings of great hostility to Europeans. Their excess of
" rights " has been again withdrawn. A recent visitor,
Adolphe Burdo, a Belgian, writes thus : " Abundantly
attired in clothes of European cut, with an umbrella in
their hands to protect their black crops of hair, the
freed-men go about nonchalantly seated in wheel chairs,
drawn by one or two negroes, their brothers, whom they
regard with disdain, and whom they treat, not like
slaves, but like beasts of burden." The natives of the surrounding country, he says, are intellectually and morally
superior to these freed negroes. Still, it must be owned
that the Sierra Leonese, when they have come under the
influence of Christianity, have apparently profited greatly,
and many of them have become clergymen and evange-
lists. There are also natives who understand trade
accounts exceedingly well, and who will have much influence in the opening up of Africa to European traffic.
Sir R. F. Burton, in his last visit to Sierra Leone, found
the state of things greatly improved.

The Republic of Liberia is the result of an American
philanthropic enterprise, originating in Washington in
Liberia. 1816, which endeavoured to make a settlement
of negroes freed in America, in their native
land, and promote its civilisation and culture by all avail-
able modes. In 1822 a territory was acquired for this
purpose, on that part of the coast of Guinea known as
the Grain or Pepper Coast, and it was named Liberia,
with high hopes that it would lead to a vast elevation

of the Africans. But it has never justified these hopes, and to a large extent it has belied them, having been unable to control the uncivilised negroes within its borders, and having been sometimes defeated by them. It is described as being in a low moral condition, oppressed by heavy taxes, with inhabitants lazy and indolent.

The Kroos, or Krumen, as they are usually called, are a native race centring in a part of Liberia, but distributed far and wide in tropical Africa, owing to their superiority as labourers. They **The Krumen.** supply gangs of labourers for ships, which are glad to engage their services notwithstanding their thieving propensities. They are known by peculiar names, such as "Tom Pepper and Bottle of Brandy," "Bottled Beer," "Prince of Wales," "I'm Bestman," "Shilling," "Sea-breeze," "Black Jack," "Full Steam"; and they look very odd at times in the peculiar travesty of European garments they adopt.

The Gold Coast, beyond Sierra Leone, is a great depository of gold, **The Gold Coast.** till lately most inefficiently worked by the natives. Now, however, the

TOM PEPPER AND BOTTLE OF BRANDY.

deposits in the valley of the Ancobra River are being well and profitably worked by British companies. Axim, the chief gold port, is a growing place, well protected, though not yet very healthy. The natives, who live in mere sheds of split bamboo fronds, are Apollonians, exhibiting, according to Burton, the usual curious compound of credulity and distrust, hope and fatalism, energy and inaction. "They are civil enough, baring the shoulders, like taking off the hat, when they meet their rulers."

They are cleanly, and feed well on an abundant meat diet, including beef, mutton, pork, and poultry. The women are ugly and plump, with hair trained into tufts, bunches, and horns. The people are much given to nicknames: children take their first name after the day of their birth, strangers after the day on which they land. The children are lively, pugnacious, and voracious.

The negroes of the coast and interior, near Cape Coast Castle, are usually spoken of as two different peoples, the Fantis and the Ashantis. This is chiefly because of their mortal hostility to one another, but they are not greatly different, except in so far as the Fantis live near and upon the coast, and have been much more influenced for good or bad by intercourse with Europeans. In some respects they have decidedly progressed; but on the whole they are not of a higher type, and are certainly not industrious. They are

FANTIS.

of a dark chocolate hue, muscular in body, with round heads, thick lips, prominent jaws, and scanty beards on the male. The women are fairly good-looking in youth, but repulsve in middle age; they are credited with more intelligence than the men, and have considerable manipulative skill.

·Both sexes wear calico garments of glaring blue, yellow, or red. All wear large waist-garments, and many cover their shoulders. The married women, in addition, wear a cushion sticking up behind, as a support for carrying a child. Girdles or strings of beads for the waist are very generally worn, and also earrings and necklaces of various forms. The hair is usually combed out long, carefully trained, and greased, and raised in a ridge, or over cushions, or twisted into one or two long horns.

Morality is of a very low type, chiefly consisting in selfishness and sensuality, among the Fantis. Even in those parts where missionary enterprise has **Moral** been most abundant, and many converts have **character.** been made, the amount of moral elevation achieved is dubious. Many of the people, fervent and zealous in their religious exercises, have little notion of carrying their religion into their daily life. Unfortunately the cost of living is so trifling that the Fanti easily lives in idleness on his wife's labour, and too frequently does so. Even when persuaded to work a little, it is done in the most leisurely fashion. Anything that can be carried on the head they will take in that way ; and there is a story that when wheelbarrows were introduced by a builder, who wanted some stones carried, the Fantis placed one stone in each barrow, and then lifted barrow and stone on to their heads, and so carried both. If any Fanti energy is to be seen, it is in dancing in peculiarly violent fashion, accompanied by loud cries. Palm-wine and rum are their favourite drinks. The usual tropical grains, fruit, and vegetables are abundant, needing scarcely any cultivation ; but a good deal of fish is caught and eaten, and even monkeys' and crocodiles' flesh is relished.

Polygamy and slavery are by no means extinct in the Fanti country, though discouraged and more or less forbidden in parts under British influence, which has in recent years been considerably extended. The old tribal divisions are still kept up, distinguished by some animal emblem. The tribal chiefs are hereditary, but the confederations elect their "king." Government **Government.** is mainly despotic and of an ignorant type, criminals being examined by ordeal. Before long, no doubt, British government will have put down the grosser injustices which prevail among them. Although the Fantis would now repel with indignation the suspicion of

CIVILISED AFRICAN.

cannibalism, it is not a century ago that it was practised, though now retained only in Ashanti and Dahomey.

Fetishism prevails very largely among the Fantis.

Fetishism. Every person has his personal fetish, which may be any ordinary or extraordinary thing, an idol of any or no form, a rag, a bunch of grass, a feather, etc. Various spirits, chiefly malevolent, are "worshipped," if such a term can be applied to their sacrifices of animal victims and the regular orgies which accompany them. The fetish festivals are kept every week, often on different days by different clans or tribes. The great annual performance is driving out the devil, which is done by a screaming and howling procession, beating drums and blowing horns, walking through every lane and valley, entering every house and banging walls and roofs, with much drinking and dancing. Witch doctors and fetish priests in abundance make their profit out of the fetish superstition, and sell charms and talismans, many of which consist simply of the teeth or claws of animals. Much new light is thrown on Fanti religious ideas by Major Ellis in his "Tshi-speaking Peoples of the Gold Coast of West Africa," 1887.

Funerals are occasions of great noise and ceremony **Burial.** when the deceased has left any pro-

WEST AFRICAN GIRL.

perty. The friends assemble before his house and yell and sing, smoke and drink, also firing guns, and sacrificing a dog and a sheep, the latter for the funeral feast. Often a good deal of personal property, even money and gold, will be buried with the body, thus affording temptation to disturb it after death, which not unfrequently happens.

The Ashantis became somewhat better known to us after our expedition to their capital in 1873; but their hostility, both to other negroes and to foreigners, is so great that we do not know very much more about them than was described by Bowdich in 1817. The capital, Kumasi, or Coomassie, dates only from about 1700, and it is supposed that both the Ashantis and the Fantis came originally from a district further north. It was built on a rocky slope almost surrounded by marshes and streams, and was an oblong about four miles round, with wide streets and open squares. The streets were all named and in charge of a superior officer; and here

ASHANTI.

and there were raised stone platforms, whence the king and his officers could survey assemblies. Markets on an extensive scale were held, at which meat and vegetables of varied kinds, with palm wine and rum, were for sale, together with beads, looking-glasses, powder, and thread, and the various manufactured articles in which negroes delight.

A CABOCEER.

The king's palace was an

K

extensive building, quite grand for Africa, with a two-
storeyed square front, flat roof and parapet, and
something like a tower. In front were a variety
of courtyards, each secured by padlocks, the number of
which formed part of the royal state. It is said to have
been designed and built by Fanti masons. The king's
furniture included a heterogeneous collection of African,
Indian, and European treasures, including pictures and
engravings, Persian rugs, red leather saddles, fine state
umbrellas, and even books in many languages. All this
palace and town were destroyed by the British army in
February, 1874; but since then a new capital has sprung
up nearly on the old site, though we have as yet no guide-
book or excursions thither, travelling being somewhat
unsafe in Ashanti, notwithstanding "British influence."

As in the case of the royal palace, the dwellings of the
people are superior to those of most African peoples.
They are made of plastered clay, the walls
being constructed in a sort of framework of
stakes. The "upper ten" have their roofs supported by
pillars, and also have verandahs similarly supported;
some have an upper storey. Their windows are made of
open woodwork, carved in fanciful patterns, and painted
red. These houses even have something like the con-
veniences of civilisation, and every morning the rubbish
and offal thrown out from the houses are burnt at the
back of the street.

Bowdich gave a glowing account of the riches, grandeur,
and state he found in Coomassie; and there is no doubt
that gold is abundant and easily obtained in
the land. But when our army visited it,
scarcely any treasures were visible or obtainable, probably
because they had been buried or safely concealed. All
the gold in the land belongs to the king, and a royal
licence is necessary for any one to wear gold ornaments.
Noisy bands of music, and the swaying and unfolding of
great umbrellas of most showy cloth and fantastically
ornamented and fringed, form a great part of the state
of the Ashanti monarch. Indeed, he seemed in Bowdich's
time to have constituted himself the central figure of all

the fine things ever sent to or made in Africa. Various animals' heads, covered with gold, were suspended from the gold-handled swords of his attendants. "Large drums, supported on the head of one man, and beaten by two others, were braced around with the thigh-bones of their enemies, and ornamented with their skulls. The kettle-drums, resting on the ground, were scraped with wet fingers and covered with leopards' skins. The wrists of the drummers were hung with bells and curiously-shaped pieces of iron, which jingled loudly as they were beating. The smaller drums were suspended from the neck by scarves of red cloth; the horns (the teeth of young elephants) were ornamented at the mouthpiece with gold and the jaw-bones of human victims. The war-caps of eagles' feathers nodded in the rear, and the large fans of the wing feathers of the ostrich played around the dignitaries. Immediately behind their chairs (which were of a black wood, almost covered by inlays of ivory and gold embossment) stood their handsomest youths, with corselets of leopards' skins, covered with gold cockle-shells, and stuck full of small knives, sheathed in

DAHOMEY WARRIOR.

gold and silver, and the handles of blue agate; cartouche-boxes of elephant's hide hung below, ornamented in the same manner; a large gold-handled sword was fixed behind the left shoulder, and silk scarves and horse-tails (generally white) streamed from the arms and waist-cloth; their long muskets had rims of gold at small distances, and the stocks were ornamented with shells. Finely-grown girls stood behind the chairs of some, with silver basins. Their stools (of the most laborious carved work, and generally with two large bells attached to them) were conspicuously placed on the heads of favourites; and crowds of small boys were seated around, flourishing elephants' tails, curiously mounted."

The king of Ashanti rules almost despotically, but the succession descends to a brother or a nephew. His power **Government.** is somewhat restricted by his captains, known as Caboceers, whom he consults on all questions of war and peace, and intercourse with foreigners. Among his great officials are the executioners, who wear great gold-hilted knives. One of them carries the death-drum, adorned with human bones, hair, and skin, and the death-block, on which some of every victim's blood is sprinkled. Human life is considered of very little consequence here, as in Dahomey. The death of a king **Human victims.** and that of his mother are marked by the sacrifice of thousands of lives; and the same is the case with every person of rank. The chief captains of the army have their bloody rites repeated for week after week. The bulk of the victims are women, slaves and criminals. Nothing can give us a darker or more terrible view of the religious state of the negro, than the realisation that this barbaric slaughter is supposed to be a necessity, in order that the dead man may be properly attended and have a suitable household. It is the exaggeration of the same feeling that is manifested in placing food for the dead to eat, and ornaments, utensils, etc., in their graves. There is so much bloodshed that there is no room for many executions for mere crime, which is lightly though strictly punished. There is no penalty for **Punishment** killing slaves; and the murder of wife or chil-**of crime.** dren is atoned by paying a fine to the wife's relatives. But a man who kills one of his own rank is condemned to kill himself. Theft is punished by a heavy fine in addition to restoration of the stolen property. No one is allowed to be out at night in Kumasi except by the king's permission. The king takes upon himself another office, that of chief fireman; at any rate it is quite the custom for him to be present at every fire.

The Ashantis are much more courageous than the Fantis, and every adult is practically a warrior, the army being elaborately organised. The common dress is a tunic of coloured calico; and the face is coated with a variety of extraordinary patterns in green and white paint. The people manufacture much of their own cloth, especially of the more gorgeous sort, using looms. They are also skilful in carpentry, leather-dressing, and iron-working.

The fetishism of the Ashanti is as elaborate and wide-reaching as their sacrifices are bloody; we must not here dilate upon the subject. Superstition is nowhere of a much lower type than among this people.

Dahomey, east of Ashanti, outdoes it in sanguinary rites. The Ffons are the negro inhabitants, ruled over by a despotic king. They are rather smaller **The Ffons** than the Ashantis, but very muscular. The **of Dahomey.** upper class are of a lighter coffee-colour than the bulk of the people. They are particularly agile in dancing and climbing trees. In character they are at once arrogant and servile, liars and boasters, cheats and thieves, blood-thirsty and vindictive, and show scarcely the semblance of affection. The women are of a stronger type than the men, though very ill-looking after their first youth; and the long pendent breasts by no means increase their beauty. Both sexes are marked with three vertical cuts on the temple. Hair is very variously dressed; and the body is kept well oiled as a protection against the heat of the sun.

The men wear a waistband, with a sort of short petti-coat above it, unless very poor. A long mantle is worn by all who can afford it, brought over the left shoulder. The women wear a similar mantle, simply wound round their bodies. Beads, rings, and other ornaments are lavishly worn, one of the strangest adornments to our ideas being a piece of candle stuck through the lobe of the ear.

The staple food is " kankey," a native bread, carefully boiled or roasted in plantain leaves. Meat is freely eaten by the well-to-do, the men being waited on by their wives on their knees. Excessive drinking is very prevalent, water being very bad and dear.

In this land all the soil is held to be the king's property, and to him rent has to be paid. The soil is very fertile, and mostly cultivated by women. The houses are inferior to those of Ashanti.

One of the most remarkable institutions of Dahomey is the famous corps of Amazons, or female soldiers. It **The Amazons.** may be that they originated in the diminution of the number of men in the country by war and executions. They are said to date from 1728, but

WIVES OF KING OF DAHOMEY.

the powerful king Gozo (1818–58) boasted that he was the first to organise the Amazons; and certainly since the early part of his reign they have formed a prominent part of the army of the king, who selects them personally from all his female subjects. A few become the king's concubines, others are married to officers, while the majority are kept in strict celibacy, on pain of death. They wear a sleeveless cotton tunic of native manufacture, striped blue and white, and short trousers.

The Amazons, as a rule, are of much finer physique than

KING GOZO (DAHOMEY) AND HIS COUNCILLORS IN GALA WAR DRESS.

the men, full of activity, of extreme courage, bold and free, and swaggering in their manner, and very formidable enemies. According to some reports, they are expert shots, loading and firing with remarkable activity; others say this is not the case. The captains carry enemies' skulls in their girdles. They are of great importance to the king's palace in performing the simple duty of fetching that rare necessary, water. They do this in single file, and strike a bell whenever any one is seen approaching, that the road may be kept clear; for in case of any accident happening to one of these women, the man who is nearest is supposed to be the cause, and loses his head or his liberty.

There is of course a considerable army of men, armed, like the Amazons, with guns and swords. Their fighting Mode of is "a system of strategy, cunning, and sur-fighting. prise; their object being to arrive at the intended point without being heard or seen. Should they succeed, so much the better for themselves; if not, they fight for an hour or two in a desultory sort of manner, without order and without discipline; after which, if they cannot carry their point, the whole army runs away, and makes the best of its way back to the capital" (Wilmot). In pursuit, the heads of enemies are chopped off without mercy. The ill-advised expedition of the Dahomans against Abeokúta in 1874 was a great failure, and greatly diminished their power.

We must not attempt to fully describe the "customs" of Dahomey, which are attended with sickening barbarity and destruction of human life. Suffice it to say, that it is alleged by the king that the victims are killed to testify his greatness in spirit-land, to send messengers to dead kings and beg their advice, and that they are criminals The or captives who are put to death. There is no customs. doubt, however, that in default of these, any subject of the king may be made to suffer a horrible death. Human skulls decorate the walls of the royal abodes; and it is even said that a sleeping room is paved with the skulls of enemies. Conquered chiefs are triumphed over by the use of their skulls as drinking-cups. The great annual customs are supposed to commemorate the king's delivery from his enemies, and they further serve the purpose of being accompanied by the payment of taxes by the subjects. The reign of terror is continually kept up by the sight of victims' heads, in various stages of decay, stuck on spikes on the earthen wall enclosing the large group of houses belonging to the king. The grand customs at a king's death are celebrated in order that the king may enter the spirit world with royal state, accompanied by numerous wives and attendants of all kinds; in these there is no pretence that criminals and enemies are put to death, unless as additions to the pomp.

Fetishism is nowhere in greater force than in Dahomey. The Ffon name for the deity in general, is Mau or ·Je-whe, far above man, and neither feared nor loved; **Fetishism.** but fetishes, able to protect human beings, or to intercede with the spirit world, are believed to reside in a great variety of objects. A certain python, Danhgbwe, not poisonous, is reputed to be the most powerful fetish, and has a common-place temple for his worship. Mr. Skertchly saw twenty-two pythons in the snake-house at Whydah (the port of Dahomey); they must not be slain, on penalty of death. There are a large number of fetish snake-priests and snake-wives. Lofty and beautiful trees are further prayed to and presented with offerings in times of sickness. The ocean is another subject of worship, and his fetish-priest at Whydah is very important, praying to the ocean-god not to be boisterous, and throwing into it rice and corn, oil and beans and cowries. The thunder-god is another great fetish. The influence of the fetish-priests is very great; and the women they collect about them are, as usual, " married to the fetish," and frequently display exciting spectacles of dancing and leaping before the people.

Fortunately Dahomey is declining in power and numbers, and it is to be hoped that a better influence will take the place of the fetish-priests. The pro- **The Yorubas** gress of Dahomey has been long resisted and **and Egbas.** barred by the people of Abeokuta, the Yorubas, further east, and the Egbas near the coast. The town of Lagos, on a lagoon island, made a British colony in 1861, has much intercourse with them, and is a great centre of trade, inhabited by a motley population. In the Yoruba country, too, Christian missionaries have had considerable success: yet the mass of people is so great that only a small portion are yet affected by reformation.

The Egbas are ugly in countenance, the women in figure also, while the bodies of the men are not wanting Physical in grace. As with other adjacent tribes, the characters. hair is dressed in fantastic patterns, and the skin tattooed with strange devices, some representing animals characterising the tribe. Coral jewellery is worn in abundance, in bangles, anklets, necklaces, and finger rings; beads of course are not forgotten.

Salutation has been developed into a fine art by this people. They have many different forms, adapted to Modes of different persons, as to a stranger, to one in the salute. house, a traveller, a person sitting, one standing, etc., and a kind of prostration is very general. Burton describes the most general way thus: after laying down whatever burden may be carried and clapping hands once, twice, or thrice, to go on all fours, touch the ground with the belly and breast, the forehead and both sides of the face successively, then kiss the earth, half rise, then pass the left over the right forearm, and *vice versâ*, and finally, after again saluting the earth, stand up. With all this ceremony, one may not be surprised to learn that the sexes eat separately.

The northern part of Yoruba has been conquered by the Fulahs, and added to the empire of Gando. Illori, a Superstitions. large town with much commerce, has a sultan, and Mahometanism is of course now the state religion. Whether human sacrifices are yet totally extinct in southern Yoruba is doubtful; but fetishism is by no means extinct, and ancestor worship is also rife. There are also several secret societies or orders performing certain rites and overawing and often tyrannising over the people. Two principal modes of influencing the superstitious are the rites of Egugun, literally " bones," supposed to be a dead man risen from the grave, and Oro, a terrific being supposed to haunt the woods, at sound of whom women must fly within doors.

We cannot particularise the multitudinous "monarchs" of the Oil Coast, the Niger delta, through which palm-oil in abundance now passes out from the interior, **The Oil** and from which vast numbers of negroes were **Coast.** formerly exported as slaves. The negroes of these coasts do not differ very greatly from one another. The king of Bonny has been a subject of jest for more than a generation, and in a few years will probably be forgotten.

GROUP OF AFRICAN PIPES.

The palm-oil coast has many rivers, known through West African trade, such as Old Calabar, New Calabar, Bonny, Brass, Benin, etc. That part of the people's character which is not silly and childish is in **Cruel** a large measure cruel and savage. Thus, Bonny **practices.** had till lately a custom of burying twins immediately after birth. In several other districts this is the practice; and also all children are killed whose upper incisors appear before the lower. As late as 1859, in the market-place of Duke Town on the Old Calabar, human flesh was exposed for sale; and in neighbouring States it is the regular practice to eat all captives in war. Ju-ju is the favourite name here for the fetish ; and every village had its great **Mumbo Jumbo.** ju-ju house with skulls and fetishes. Mumbo Jumbo is a common object of terror and discipline, parallel to Egugun and Oro, who appears as a figure in fantastic and horrible garb, and who at various festivals seizes on some woman or other person who has offended public opinion, and administers a severe thrashing.

The tribes of the Lower Niger are very hostile to Europeans, the chiefs asserting their right to levy heavy toll **The people of Abo.** on all merchandise passing into or out of the country, and preventing direct intercourse, in order to make a greater profit. Abo is one of the most populous centres ; but the people are very treacherous, although for the most part poor. They really subsist largely upon piracy. Chiefs are elected by fierce contests, and the victor puts his rivals to death.

PREPARING A FERNANDO PO BRIDEGROOM.

The Abo men are easily recognised, says Burdo, by their being tattooed with three parallel incisions on the temples from the eye to the ear lobe, and three others horizontally above the nose and between the eyes. The women have a greater number of incisions. All are loaded with heavy rings of ivory or copper on arms and legs ; and the women wear their anklets after marriage as a sort of wedding ring, never removed. Many of them are copper-coloured, fine men, well-grown and having blue eyes. They talk a great deal, and are very ferocious in argument, and easily pass to extremes. A cannibal race among them is very much darker, lean, bony, and miserable-looking.

Marriage among these people is a mere commercial transaction, with little or no ceremony. The women have no notion of modesty or of coquetry. Every wife a man has becomes his slave. They do a great deal of work, and are even sent about the country to collect palm-oil and ivory. They do not carry their infants on their backs or on their hips, but in their arms. Children only stay with their parents so long as they cannot provide for themselves ; the moment they can do this they take flight, except in the case of a chief's or rich man's family. There is a class of agriculturists among them who have good plantations of yams, bananas, and maize, and are active, industrious, and intelligent.

The slave market at Igbebe, just south of the junction of the Niger and the Benué, says M. Burdo, is the saddest sight in the world. " Just like beasts of burden, men, women, and children are publicly exposed quite naked, to be sold to the highest bidder. The slave-dealer does his best to show off their good qualities, and the buyer, in his turn, subjects them to a minute and critical examination. Among other things, he looks into their mouths to see the state of their teeth ; and this examination is submitted to without the least recoil. The price of men varies not only with strength, looks, and age, but also with the district from which they come, according as the people have a peaceable or spiteful and vindictive reputation.

In these essentially negro lands, as among so many other races, the priest and the king rule savagely by force and by terror, and ignorance and superstition hang over the land. Yet elements of progress are discernible —the most evil races are dying out, the traffic in slaves is diminishing, the Mahometan governments which have spread over such large tracts are certainly less evil than those which they have replaced, and in some parts Christian missionaries have exerted an influence which not all the drunkenness and vice promoted by traders or immoral travellers have outweighed. Still, Europeans, if by them the problem is to be solved, have very much yet to do before their methods become properly adapted to redeem the African from barbarism and make him a decent member of civilised society.

We must briefly refer to the Islands of the Gulf of Guinea, of which Fernando Po, belonging to Spain, is the chief. It is used by Spain as a place of exile for political offenders; but is also in-habited by tribes of negroes derived from the mainland, who call themselves Boubi, or, as English sailors will have it, "Boobies," signifying however simply "The Men." They speak at least five different Bantu dialects. They are shorter and less muscular than the continental negroes, and are comparatively timid and gentle. They are deeply gashed in various parts of the body, and coat themselves with red clay and palm oil. Rubbing chins is a favourite mode of salutation among them. Usually they wear little but a straw hat, and are very unwilling to adopt civilised habits or to mix freely with Europeans or strangers. They worship a great spirit whom no one can see, but who is revealed by a dazzling light and by a voice issuing from the ground. His priest is established in a cave, and transmits prayers to the spirit. Annobon, another small Spanish island, has 3000 negro inhabitants who profess Roman Catholi-cism. Saint Thomas, a Portuguese island just north of the Equator, is inhabited chiefly by Angola negroes, who grow coffee and cocoa in large quantities. Numerous colonists from Brazil have also settled there.

The Portuguese gave the name "Camaraos," meaning "shrimps," to the many-branched estuary in the north-east of the Bight of Biafra, south-east of the great volcanic mass now known as the Cameroon Mountains, close to the coast. The name Cameroons is now applied to the German territory which includes this mountain mass; it has great importance, as including extensive possible habitats for Europeans. The southern limit of the German possessions on the coast is the River Campo. So far as known, nearly all the inhabitants speak Bantu languages, and they are described as civilised. They are divided into a great number of small disunited tribes, the best known of which are the Bakuiri, the Bakundu, the Dualla, and the Bakoko. The former are remarkable for the small size of the women, while the

WOMEN OF THE GABOON RIVER.

men are above the average height of the neighbouring tribes. They are a very intelligent and active people, good hunters and soldiers, living around the German settlements at Victoria and Bimbia. They are notable for their popular assemblies, in which they show great oratorical skill; they also sing and recite, and have a good deal of sentiment. There is a considerable tribal *esprit de corps* among them. Sorcery and the tyranny of fetish-priests have full sway, and there is a good deal of ancestor-worship.

The Bakundu are a very industrious people, living on the north side of the Cameroons, having stone houses, **The Bakundu.** frequently painted with representations of animals and men. They have a large assembly-house, which also serves as a slaughter-house. Tanning, mat, basket, and net making, are among the pursuits in which they are skilful. They are in constant communication with the peoples to the north, and are acquainted with the Fulahs and the Arabs. Slaves are abundant among them, bought from the North, and living in separate communities.

The Dualla have some features of resemblance to Europeans and Semites, but they are as dark-coloured as their neighbours. The calves of their legs **The Dualla.** are more developed than in most African races. Children mature early, and boys marry and set up as traders at nine or ten. Women are simply regarded as chattels, and are often brought up by rich men and chiefs for use or sale. The Dualla and several neighbouring peoples have invented a system of telegraphing by means of their drums, every mode and succession of drum-strokes representing a distinct sound, or a syllable. These messages, when heard by the initiated, are at once repeated by them, and thus in a very short time news is transmitted through the country. Slaves are not allowed to learn this sign-language. Cannibalism was practised till recent times amongst them, and each seizure of power was preceded by a murder. The chiefs are very wealthy, taking toll of all merchandise entering, leaving, or passing through their domains. Palm-oil, palm-nuts, and ivory are the chief articles of export.

From 1470 onwards, the Portuguese visited Africa south of the Equator, and many capes, rivers, etc., still bear **The Gaboon and Ogoway.** Portuguese names; but exploration in the Gaboon country only began in 1842, when the French acquired a small territory on the north side of the Gaboon estuary. Subsequently the expeditions of M. Du Chaillu (1856, 1865) and his marvellous stories of gorilla-land made the locality famous. Still more recently the large river Ogoway was explored by travellers of several nations. From 1875 onwards, M. de Brazza, with numerous assistants, has been engaged in opening up the whole district from the Gaboon to the Congo. All the people speak Bantu languages.

The Mpongwé are the most civilised and numerous inhabitants. The language is remarkable for its extent and precision ; and, owing to this, it has been The Mpon-possible to translate the Gospels into it without gwé. using a single foreign word. The people appear to have accommodated themselves to Christianity with consider-able ease, and have adopted Sabbath observance with great enthusiasm, decking themselves in absurd finery on that day. One great sign of importance among them is the possession of a large bunch of keys, suspended from the neck, supposed to indicate the number of chests of valuables which they possess. In many ways they imitate European customs, although they by no means diminish the number of their wives. In the inland region of Galoa, some distance up the Ogoway, these people are found in full vigour and intelligence, with handsome women who have their secret societies, by means of which they gain considerable power. Al-though Mahometanism has not penetrated so far, circum-cision is practised among several tribes.

The Bakalais are a tribe inhabiting the forests of the interior, chiefly south of the Ogoway. Like the Mpongwé they are diminishing, especially under the The Bakalais. attacks of the Fans. They are very prone to migrate, having a great fear of death ; when two persons die within a few days, they believe the settlement is be-witched, and hurriedly abandon it. Like many other tribes in the Gaboon country, the young men marry out of their own village, and if possible out of their tribe. On a man's death, his son succeeds to his wives, with the exception of his own mother. Their food is largely derived from the manioc, dressed with vegetable oil. Very few fish are caught, and they have no domestic animals. Moreover, such animals as might supply food are tabooed, elephant to one, monkey to another, crocodile to another ; but the craving for animal food becomes uncontrollable at times, and accounts for much cannibalism. In late years these people have had the wit to adapt themselves to circumstances, and become merchants and carriers for their European superiors.

The Fans are in every way a more powerful people,

FAN BARGAINING FOR A BRIDE.

living just north and south of the Equator, east of the
The Fans. Gaboon, and north of the Ogoway. They have progressed steadily from the East, and are crushing the feebler people between them and the coast.

They are rapidly increasing, their women being very fertile, which is attributed to their marrying later than the women of the coast tribes. Their language is a Bantu one, though with numerous peculiarities. They have been said to belong to the same stock physically as the Niam-Niam, having also several of the same customs, including cannibalism. The men are soldiers and hunters, muscular and lean, proud and self-confident. Their lips are comparatively thin, and the jaws are not as prominent as in most negroes. The women perform all drudgery and household work, and are very ugly after youth. In both sexes the forehead is very rounded above the eyebrows. Personal ornament is much valued. Tattooing, painting, necklaces, feathers, cowry-shells, are greatly in vogue. Copper rings round the calves remind one of East African tribes. Some women are so heavily loaded with ornaments that they cannot walk.

Cannibalism, universal among the Fans when first known, is diminishing in all those who have come near European influence. Prisoners of war and sorcerers are still eaten in the interior; and in some cases the

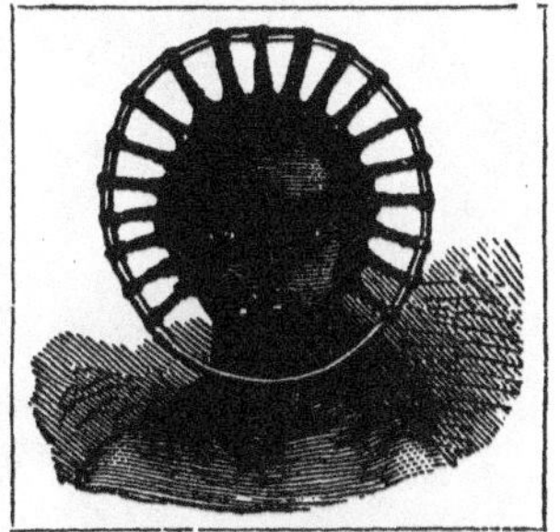

ASHIRA BELLE, SOUTH OF OGOWAY.

cannibal feasts have a religious character. As they have come in contact with trade and people from the coast, they have begun to settle down as agriculturists, boatmen, and merchants. Their general intelligence is shown by the variety of occupations they take up. They include skilful blacksmiths, ebony bow-makers, potters, and gardeners.

The gorillas which inhabit the Fan country are feared by the Fans, though they hunt and kill them. A gorilla skull is kept, among others, in the fetish-house of each village, and treated as a sacred object.

South of the Ogoway, the Ashira are among the notable tribes, being renowned for the good looks of their women.

This, is in fact, leading to their decrease, for the Bakalai

The Ashira. and other tribes buy or steal them. Smallpox also has played a destructive part in diminishing the people. Ashira women enjoy a considerable status, may own property, and are consequently well treated. These people remove the two middle upper incisors and

THE ORDEAL OF THE HOT RING, WEST AFRICA.

file the other teeth. Their hair is dressed in extraordinary forms. They have very decent villages, with paths between them, and many patches of cultivated ground. They are very fond of palm wine, and of smoking a species of Indian hemp. Fetishism flourishes among them, but they have the habit of choosing their doctors from other tribes than their own. Du Chaillu gives an account of one of their ordeals which we may quote. A man accused of injuring another man's canoe, was subjected to the ordeal of the ring boiled in oil. "The Ashira doctor," he says, "set three little billets of bar wood in the ground with their ends together, then piled some smaller pieces between them. A native pot, half-filled with palm oil, was set upon the wood, and the oil was set on fire. When it burned up brightly, a brass ring from the doctor's hand was cast into the pot. The doctor stood by with a little vase full of grass, soaked in water, of which he threw in now and then some bits. This made the oil blaze up afresh. At last all was burnt out, and now came the trial. The accuser, a little boy, was required to take the ring out of the pot; he hesitated, but was pushed on by his father. The people cried out, 'Let us see if he lied or told the truth.' Finally, he put his hand in, seized the red-hot ring, but quickly dropped it, having severely burnt his fingers. At this there was a shout, 'He lied, he lied!' and the man accused was declared innocent."

Another singular custom is exposing the dead in the open air. At the obsequies of a chief, at which Du Chaillu was present, the corpse was placed on the ground in a sitting posture, enveloped in a large European coat, and with an umbrella by his side (both given him by the explorer); by his side was a chest containing various presents and favourite possessions, also a plate of victuals, which was renewed daily for some time; and a fire was kept burning near by. All around were the bones of previous chiefs in various stages of decay.

The Obongo are a dwarf race, dwelling in the forests south of the Ogoway, sheltered in huts of leafy branches, often hidden in depressions of the ground, or **The Obongo.** among rocks. They are a timid people, living on berries, and such game as they can catch in pit-falls. They are yellowish-brown in complexion, and have low retreating foreheads, high cheek-bones, and short tufted hair. Their legs are short relatively to the body, which is rarely more than four feet seven in height. They rarely have any clothing, and their huts are full of vermin, and have an intolerable stench. Their little communities, of about a dozen, marry exclusively within their own limits. They dispose of the dead at once by throwing them into a river bed or the trunk of a tree. They excite no hostility among the neighbouring tribes, who, on the contrary, whenever they see them, are very kind to them and make them presents. Whether they are related to the Akka described in a former chapter, cannot yet be settled, but it seems quite possible.

Here, between the French and the Portuguese possessions, we must draw the boundary line of our chapter. South of this region the great Congo district begins, and we are launched into Southern Africa.

CHAPTER VIII.

The South Africans.

History of Cape Colony—Rivalry of Dutch and English—Sheep and ostrich farming—The diamond fields—The natives—Malays—Coolies—The Hottentots—Dwellings—Manners and customs—Government—Religion—The Hottentot language—The Bushmen—To whom related?—Physical characters—Mode of life—Rock carvings and drawings—The digging-stick—Forlorn condition—The Bantu peoples—Bantu languages—Bantu divisions—The Zulu Kaffirs—Rise of Chaka—Foundation of Natal—Cetewayo—Offshoots of the Zulus—Matabele and other kingdoms—The Kaffir kraal—Clothing—Ornaments—Food—Herding and hunting—Condition of women—Marriage—Children—Manufactures—Morals and intellect—Amusements—Government—Superstitions—The Amakhosa—The Basutos—The Bechuanas—Superstitions—The linyakas—The moloi—Influence of Christianity—Future of the natives.

BUSHMAN.

ALTHOUGH it was discovered by the Portuguese navigator, Bartholomew Diaz, in 1486, and first named by him Cape of Storms, and afterwards Cape of Good Hope by the king of Portugal, from its affording a good hope of a sea route to the Indies, the Portuguese failed to make permanent settlements at the Cape. The Dutch settled there in 1652, and gave the name of Hottentots to the natives. Cape Town was founded by Dutch and German farmers, to whom many Huguenot

History of Cape Colony.

refugees were added after the revocation of the Edict of
Nantes. The Dutch gradually extended their territory,
driving the Hottentots further afield, and enslaving many
of them. The Dutch colonial government was so pedantic
and tyrannical that it caused many of the settlers to remove further and further into the interior, thus introducing that system of "trekking" which exists to the
present day, and which is combined with resistance to
authority and sharp practice in dealing with the natives.
In 1795, the Cape colonists declared themselves an independent republic ; but the British came to the rescue,
and kept the colony under for the Dutch at first, and
after 1806 for themselves. Up to this time negro slaves
had been regularly imported from other parts of Africa,
as well as Malays from the East ; but in 1807 the import
trade was stopped, and in 1834 all negroes were emancipated. Meanwhile many acts of injustice by the Boers,
as the descendants of the Dutch farmers were called, had
led to struggles with the Kaffirs, and eventually to British
wars with them in various tracts, all resulting disastrously
for the natives, who have been steadily driven out or
hemmed in. At the same time the Boers were dissatisfied
with British rule, and began to remove and establish independent communities beyond the British borders. Thus
were founded the Orange River Free State, the Transvaal
Republic, Natal, Griqualand West, and Griqualand East.
In 1842, the British took possession of Natal ; and in
recent years all Griqualand has been similarly appropriated. The attempt, made in 1877, to annex the
Transvaal to the British possessions failed to content the
Boers ; and after determined and often successful defence
of their positions against British troops in 1881, they
again obtained the recognition of their internal independence, on condition of giving up foreign relations to the
Queen as Suzerain. But judging by past history, it
appears inevitable that small independent States in South
Africa should be absorbed in a stronger power.

Cape Colony, which received a representative constitution in 1853, has a population of which only about one-
fifth are of European descent, chiefly British and Dutch,

many of the latter speaking Dutch as well as English. The greatest difficulties of the colony arise, **Rivalry of** and have arisen, from jealousies between the **Dutch and** Dutch and the English, largely due to the fact **English.** that the latter succeeded to control of the colony after nearly two centuries of Dutch rule, and that they have imposed restrictions on Dutch treatment of natives. (The idea that thrashing and even killing a native was a crime, was most unpalatable to the former generation of Dutch-

men, and its enforcement has led to a very bitter feeling against the English. The losses associated with the abolition of slavery have increased this. Moreover, the self-assertion and bounce of a large proportion of English settlers was very offensive to the phlegmatic but still resentful Dutch. Thus there has been comparatively little of that intermarriage between the two groups which might have smoothed matters, and a great deal of inter-mixture with natives which has really lowered the latter, and has developed a type of idle hanger-on to the settler, by no means morally reputable. Still, as Mr. Stanley Little says in his " South Africa," " English capital and English brains have supplied South Africa with its railways, its harbours, its public buildings, and all its industries, with the exception of sheep-farming and wine-producing. England has protected the colonies from savages within and without their boundaries ; English ships convey African produce to profitable markets." But it is absurd and wrong for the Englishman to sneer at his Dutch rival of African birth by calling him an Africander, too often with improper epithets. Too many who have gone to the Cape with the idea of winning money and diamonds easily, have expected to find every man their servant, even those of European descent. It is to be hoped that in a few years this race antagonism will be mitigated, otherwise fresh troubles will arise.

Cape Town, Port Elizabeth, Graham's Town, Graaf Reinet, and Kimberley are the largest towns—the latter a mushroom growth of a few years. The first two are of considerable size, and have many handsome buildings. Their population is very mixed, the Dutch being in largest numbers in Cape Town. But the great bulk of the colony is but sparsely peopled by either Europeans or natives. The sheep and ostrich farms are of great extent, and the colony produces a vast amount of wool and ostrich feathers. The ostriches are carefully nurtured, and their feathers are regularly clipped off, not plucked, as they reach maturity. The eggs even are artificially hatched. Wine-making is now steadily developing. Copper mining is an extensive industry on the western side of the colony, in Little Namaqua Land. But the most remarkable development in recent years has been that of the diamond fields in Griqualand West, extending over an area almost as large as Switzerland. The first diamond was found only in 1867 ; but in a few years a large population was collected in the " dry " and river diggings. The usual phenomena of rushes to new places, sudden fortunes, sudden ruin, wild drinking and gambling, set in; but Kimberley has now become a permanent city with stone buildings, churches, hotels, etc.

To give here a general idea of the South African natives they may be broadly divided into Hottentots and Bush-men, and members of the Bantu family, of whom the Kaffirs are a leading type. The *The natives.* former appear to have been the earlier inhabitants, and to have been driven further and further south by the latter, who now extend from Lake Victoria Nyanza and the Congo right down to Natal and Caffraria. Both these types are markedly distinct from the Equatorial Negro. We must note, however, the presence of about ten thousand Malays (originally Dutch slaves from Borneo and Sumatra) in Cape Town and Port *Malays.* Elizabeth, who supply a large proportion of the artisans, bricklayers, carpenters, tailors, coachmen, etc., and even skilful fishermen, while their wives are washer-women. They are Mahometans, having been converted while in Africa by missionaries from Mecca, and have good mosques where the festivals are well kept. They bear a very good character in general, are happy, social, sober, and respect-ful. The men wear large quaint hats of straw, resembling the top of a pagoda. The women usually wear bright garments and are not veiled.

These are not all the imported natives of the Cape, for the British have introduced more than ten thousand coolies from India, to do the farm and other labour, especially in Natal. They are intelli- *Coolies.* gent and civil, yet often dishonest and cunning.

The Hottentots (in their own tongue Quæ-quæ or Khoi-khoin—that is, " men ") now number about ninety thou-sand (though many of these show intermixture *The* with European and other races), divided into *Hottentots.* three main groups, the Namaquas, Korannas, and Griquas. They are of medium height, and have a yellowish-brown complexion, and very frizzly hair, growing more or less in tufts. Their narrow foreheads and small chins, com-bined with wide cheek-bones, give their face a somewhat lozenge-shaped appearance. They have thick everted lips, and broad flat nostrils.

It is difficult now to find Hottentots who have not been more or less influenced by Europeans. It is consequently best to describe them in the main according to the account of Peter Kolbe, who lived at the Cape in the early part of the last century. Naturally they are rather good-looking, but soon lose their looks and become coarse and wrinkled. The women, after having borne children, have very pendulous breasts, and they early acquire a striking development of fat in the sitting quarter, which is expansive enough to enable children to stand upon it and be carried in that posture. The men, though now-a-days they have adopted European fashions, formerly wore little but sheep, wild cat, or tiger skins round their shoulders and loins, according to their rank, which they wore winter and summer, day and night. Hanging from their necks were pouches containing knives, pipes, tobacco, etc., and on their arms were ivory rings. The women, in addition to garments of skins, wore aprons from which ornaments hung down. Victuals were carried in a bag hung round the neck. Both body and head were plentifully besmeared with grease, often mixed with a reddish iron paint.

Hottentot villages, or kraals, were situated on pasture land, the beehive huts being arranged in circles. The **Dwellings.** entire village was readily and frequently removed to another site. The women did all the household work, and ate apart from the men. The huts were very simply furnished with a few earthen vessels, tortoise-shell spoons and dishes, and calabashes and skins for holding milk and butter. A hole in the middle held the fire; slight excavations on either side of the hearth formed beds. Cows' and ewes' milk, buffalo and other meat, wild roots and fruits were the chief foods.

The adult youth was marked by incisions on his body by his elders, and received additional cuts when he killed **Manners and** an elephant, hippopotamus, or rhinoceros. **customs.** Marriage was arranged by a suitor with the bride's parents; and the accepted suitor, with his kindred, drove several fat oxen to their home, and killed them for the wedding feast. The priest afterwards ratified the

"OUTSPAN": SOUTH AFRICAN TRAVELLING, THE OXEN UNYOKED.

marriage by sprinkling the pair. Polygamy and divorce were more or less prevalent. Sons used to take the mother's family name, and daughters that of the father. Parents treated their children kindly, and the latter were respectful to their parents; but old people were not unfrequently exposed and left to die; some say this was only when food was scarce. But, on the whole, they were characterised by mutual affection and gentleness, with great hospitality. They were and are indolent, and inactive in every way except in hunting and looking after their cattle. Hunting, as well as war, was pursued with the assegais, bows and poisoned arrows, and sticks with

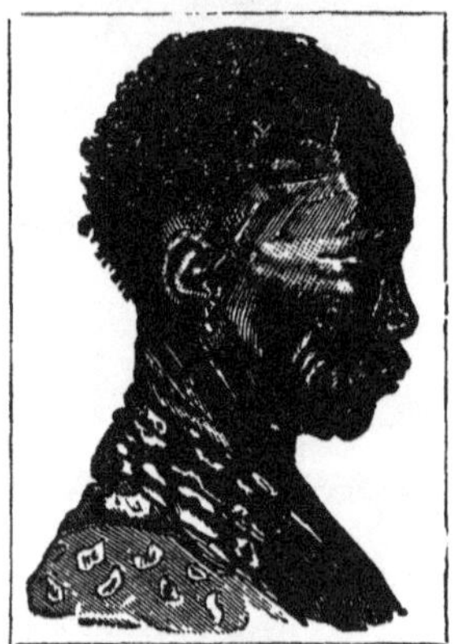

HOTTENTOT WOMAN.

large knobs at one end. Feasting, smoking, dancing, and singing formed their principal amusements, to which may now be added in not a few cases, drinking "Cape smoke," a fiery spirit. They had a few peculiar musical instruments, partly stringed, partly wind. Their dances are kept up with great endurance, sometimes through a whole night, with clapping of hands and various odd contortions of body. Sometimes any recent occurrence is described, with appropriate actions, at great length, and with much freedom of language.

This simple people had a patriarchal form of government, now almost completely superseded by British rule.

Government. There was a chief of each tribe and a captain of each kraal, and these met in council on important matters. A part of every animal taken in hunting was given to the chief, who was treated with considerable reverence. The captains of each kraal settled disputes and dealt with crime, with the co-operation of the men of his kraal. Murder and theft, especially cattle stealing, were severely punished.

A large number of nature and spirit deities were held

in regard, but a kind of ancestor-worship was actively maintained. The chief deified hero, Heitsi-Ibib, was believed to have been a great warrior, *Religion.* once the ruler of the Hottentots, who came from the East. By this fact the Namaquas accounted for their huts opening towards the east, and their graves being placed east and west, with the deceased's face looking towards the east. Ghosts were driven away by various ceremonies, and charms were much believed in, together with witch-doctors.

Stolid, not very sensitive to pain, very impatient of restraint and continuous work, the Hottentots cannot be said to have in them the makings of a nation. Although not a few of them have shown themselves capable of elevation by Christianity, the majority remain but moderately advanced in civilisation and intelligence. Many of them are described as lazy, untruthful, without a thought beyond the present, and capable of any crime for the sake of fire-water.

The Hottentot language, which has several dialects, is remarkable for its "click" sounds, almost unpronounceable by Europeans, being chiefly uttered in draw- *The Hottentot* ing in the breath, and comparable to the sound *language.* used to urge on horses, the crack of a whip, and the popping of a cork. It is said that three-fourths of their syllables begin with these clicks, which are produced by the tongue applied to the gums or roof of the mouth, and suddenly withdrawn. Europeans cannot readily follow these clicks immediately with another syllable, as do the Hottentots. There are also several hard and deep guttural and nasal sounds in this language. It has a regular grammatical structure, with pronoun suffixes of a complex type, and in some features even suggesting a resemblance to the Hamitic languages, as if they had been originally one, but separated at a later period by the intervening Negro and Bantu peoples.

There has been considerable controversy as to the Bushmen, a poor and dwindling race of outcasts, *The Bushmen.* who live a miserable life among rocks and in caves in the mountains of the Cape Colony and deserts further north. Their name is derived from the Dutch "Bosjesmans," men of the woods, whom they treated as almost brutes, without mercy or kindness. Although some features suggest their distinctness from the Hottentots, we are compelled to admit that there is no anatomical or physiognomical reason for separating them. They are simply a smaller and more infantile type of the same race. They average between four feet six to eight inches in height; and the skull, though exceeding in cranial capacity that of the Andamanese and the Veddas, is small and moderately long-headed. It is oblong-shaped with straight sides, vertical forehead, and largely developed occipital region. The cheek-bones project considerably, but there are no marked superorbital ridges. The noses are very flat and nostrils wide; in fact, they have the flattest and widest nostrils of any race. They are by no means markedly prognathous, or forward-jawed. In this and in some other characters, Prof. Flower regards them as recalling the infantine condition of the true Negro.

To whom related? Many of the disputes about Bushmen no doubt arise from their varying condition in different localities, and from the fact that outcast nomads have originated from various tribes. But there are some distinctions still unexplained, and it may be that some of them have blended with Kaffir and Hottentot tribes, and so have become modified. Their language differs considerably from the Hottentot, having no fewer than six click sounds, while the Hottentots have but four, and the Kaffirs three. The theory has been advanced, that the Bushmen were an aboriginal race in South Africa, whom first the Hottentots, and later the Kaffirs, drove into retreat. In any case, however, the anatomical resemblance to Hottentots proves that they cannot be other than nearly related to them.

The blackened grease with which the Bushmen smear themselves renders their apparent colour much darker **Physical characters.** than it really is. They are of a yellowish colour, not unlike Mongoloids; but the hair, like that of the Hottentots, is apt to assume a tufted appearance. Their protruding stomachs, hollowed-out back, prominent posteriors, and small limbs, together with the cunning and distrustful eyes and movable eyebrows, nostrils, corners of mouth, and ears, render these outcasts very repulsive. Altogether, they are of a very degraded type and habits. One of them is thus described by Lichtenstein : " When a piece of meat was given him, he snatched it hastily, and stuck it immediately into the fire, peering around with his little keen eyes, as if fearing lest some one should take it away again; all this was done with such looks and gestures that any one must have been ready to swear he had taken example of them entirely from an ape. He soon took the meat from the embers, wiped it hastily with his right hand upon his left arm, and tore out half-raw bits with his teeth."

In dress the Bushmen essentially resemble the Hottentots. Their dwellings are sometimes reed huts, but frequently mere holes in the ground or shelters **Mode of life.** arranged among the rocks by hanging mats on the windward side. Neither agriculture nor cattle-rearing are found among them, hunting being their chief resource. In this pursuit they display qualities which suggest to us very strikingly an early condition of mankind. With senses sharpened by living at war with the animal creation, eyes keen as a hawk's, ears of extraordinary acuteness, scent like that of a dog, they protect themselves against and even kill the lion and leopard, striking them with their small arrows poisoned with a mixture of vegetable and snake or other animal poisons carefully prepared. Thus equipped, the Bushmen can master the larger wild animals; but the ostrich is more difficult to stalk, being so completely on the alert in his open desert haunts. Yet the art of the Bushman is adequate, for he decks himself with an ostrich's skin, and otherwise gets himself up so as to deceive the animal, and come unperceived within range. These various hunting arts have rendered the Bushman also a clever cattle-thief; and consequently the Kaffirs, Hottentots, and Boers hold him in detestation, the latter never hesitating to kill him when within reach: but to hunt him has proved the destruction of many a man who could not vie in acuteness of senses and fertility of stratagem and ambush with the wild native, whose poisoned arrows frequently did their deadly work.

Another characteristic of Bushmen affords a suggestive theme. They are very fond of carving their rocky abodes **Rock carvings** with drawings of men, women, and children, **and drawings.** or of animals in illustrative attitudes, thus reminding one of the cave men of early European times. They are chiefly upon sandstone, in ochre of various colours, and the outlines cut with triangular pieces of flint. There are also rings, crosses, and representations of the heavenly bodies drawn in blue pigment on some of the rocks; and in various respects these remind us of primitive Egyptian signs. Another peculiarity of the Bushmen is the use of a rude digging-stick, a sharpened piece of hard wood, over which a heavy perforated stone **The digging-** is passed, and fixed by a wedge. These are **stick.** used in digging for succulent tuberous roots of desert plants, the weight of the stone being of service in driving the point of the stick into the ground, and also as a fulcrum in digging out the tuber. Similar bored stones have been found far and wide in South Africa, indicating the former area of the race which used them.

It is impossible not to compassionate the forlorn condition of the Bushmen. With scarcely an amusement or a **Forlorn** comfort, with few ideas but those of vengeance **condition.** and eating, with no regular government, with the most rudimentary kind of marriage—it being stated that they have no word to express the difference between a married and an unmarried woman—with but little even of superstition, still less of religion, these people have been like the children of Ishmael, and are among those races whom we must regard as sad comments upon the inexorable law of the struggle for existence.

Before dealing with the remaining South African peoples in detail, we will describe some of the common character- **The Bantu** istics of the larger portion of them, known now **peoples.** as Bantu, within which the Kaffirs Zulus, Bechuanas, Damaras, and most of the Congo and Zambesi tribes are included. They have a cranial capacity much above that of the average Negro and the Hottentot. The

KAFFIR WAGGON AND TEAM.

form of the nostrils and the projection of the nose are
those characteristic of the Negro race; the skull is long
and high, but their jaws do not project forward to the
same extent, being intermediate between the Negro and
the European, and the teeth being comparatively small.
Thus physically, while truly Negroes, they are a distinct
subdivision.   Moreover, they have languages as peculiar
Bantu as any group of peoples, but so alike among
languages. themselves that they must all have sprung
from one common stock.   The Hottentot " clicks " are
partially used in only the Kaffir groups; but the Bantu
languages are remarkable for their system of inflexions
being prefixed to words, at the same time that a number
of these inflexions may be added together at the beginning.   Thus the prefix U to a tribe-name indicates a
country, Wa the people of the country, M an individual,
and Ki the language.   Abantu is the term, signifying
men, by which the Kaffirs designate themselves (Kaffir,
meaning heathen, being the name originally applied by
Persians to the non-Mahometan inhabitants of " Kaffiris-
tan," and adopted by Portuguese, Dutch, and English
successively, from hearing it used on the east coast of
Africa); and it has been simplified to Bantu and taken
to indicate the entire group of peoples allied to the
Kaffirs.   The Bantu languages have something like two
hundred and fifty different forms for the verb, expressing
every variety of relation.   Altogether, they are among
the most highly complex forms of speech, yet are regular
and harmonious in structure, and with a sort of alliterative
concordance running through each sentence, thus constituting, as Mr. Kèane says, " one of the most astonishing
phenomena in the history of human culture " (" Encyclo-
pædia Britannica," 9th ed., vol. xiii., p. 821).

The Bantu as a rule are dark brown, with an infusion
of red   Their hair is not so frizzly as that of the
Bantu equatorial negro.   In mental character they
divisions. are much in advance of their darker brethren;
and their body corresponds, being robust and vigorous.
The Eastern Bantu may be divided into the Kaffir, the
Zambesi and Nyassa, and the Swahili or Zanzibar groups.

The first of these is the most important, including as it does the Zulus, the Khosa, the Pondos, the Fingoes, the Tembu, Matabele, etc. It will be best to deal with these in a general way, for, in fact, their tribes and nations are but temporary groupings brought about by the predominance of some chief or dynasty. Thus Ama-Khosa means Khosa's people, dating from a chief named Khosa, who lived perhaps **The Zulu** about three **Kaffirs.** hundred years ago. The Zulus are the people of Zulu's land, and believe themselves to have been founded by Zulu. Chaka, the celebrated chief of the Zulus, supposed to be seventh in descent from Zulu, distinguished himself early in the present century by his valour and daring, and excited his father's jealousy so greatly, that the youth fled from him. Coming into contact with Europeans, he was greatly interested in hearing from them about the formation of soldiers into regiments, and the discipline of armies. On his father's death, in 1813, he became chief of **Rise of** his tribe, put to death those hostile to him, **Chaka.**

KAFFIR YOUNG MAN WITH KNOBKERRIES.

and began to extend his dominion. His people he made a nation of soldiers, by persevering and cruel discipline; and before he died he conquered, or forced into alliance with himself, the whole south-eastern region of Africa, from the river Limpopo to Cape Colony. But this rule was attended with terrible massacres, not only of conquered people, but of his own subjects; among the most terrible of these was that which took place at the funeral of Chaka's mother, when seven thousand fell, and ten of the best-looking girls were buried alive with her. In 1838 Chaka was murdered, and was succeeded by his brother, Dingaan, who was not less bloody nor less tyrannical. Dingaan having treacherously killed a number of Dutch Boers who had come "trekking" from Cape Colony, and whom he

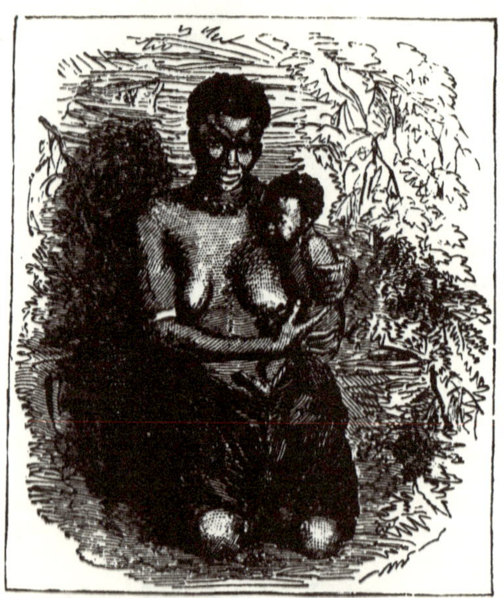

KAFFIR WOMAN AND CHILD.

had invited to settle in his land, the Dutch leader Pretorius was able to defeat and depose him, and to set up his brother Panda as chief. These Boers founded the colony of Natal; but in 1843 they were subdued by British troops, who made Natal a British colony.

In 1856, during Panda's life, a great battle was fought between his rival sons, Cetewayo (Ketchwayo), and

KAFFIRS IN FRONT OF HUT.

Umbulazi, in which the latter was defeated. In 1872
Cetewayo. Cetewayo succeeded his father, and at first he
maintained a friendly attitude to the British.
The history of his later hostility and of the Zulu war is
well known, as well as the downfall of his power at the
battle of Ulundi, in 1879, when he was made prisoner.
It cannot be said that conspicuous wisdom has been displayed in the subsequent treatment either of the king
(since dead) or of his people. Zululand has been annexed
by Great Britain, except a portion forming the "New
Republic," established by Boers in Western Zululand.

Chaka's success and discipline had wide-reaching con-
sequences. Various captains of his armies grew ambitious,
Offshoots of and set up for themselves, forming consider-
the Zulus. able kingdoms which absorbed many tribes.
Thus Umselekatse occupied the present Transvaal territory, driving out the feebler Bechuanas, and being in
turn driven out by the Boers, and settling further north
and forming the Matabele kingdom between the Limpopo
and the Zambesi. His successor, Lo Benguela, began his
reign in 1870. Another of Chaka's generals, Manikoos,
Matabele after failing to expel the Portuguese from
and other Delagoa Bay, subjugated the tribes between
kingdoms. the Limpopo and the Lower Zambesi, and
founded the kingdom of Gasa. Chaka's influence extended
beyond his own kingdom, inducing Sebituane, chief of
the Makololo (Basutos), to adopt his military system; his
kingdom, near the source of the Vaal, passed northwards
to the Zambesi and the east of the Kalahari desert, but
after attaining considerable power, was destroyed by the
subjugated tribes of the Barotse. The Maviti, whose
conquests about Lakes Nyassa and Tanganyika have been
described by Livingstone, appear to be another branch
of Chaka's Zulus. Among all these peoples military
despotism is the prevailing phenomenon. "Matabele
society," says Mr. Mackenzie, "may be said to exist for the
chief. His claims are supreme and unquestioned. To
him belongs every person and everything in the country."

Amatongaland is another of these Zulu kingdoms
north of Zululand, and extending to Delagoa Bay. It

has a queen and many subordinate chiefs. Swaziland is yet another adjacent Zulu kingdom.

Devoting a short space now to the habits and customs of some of the several types of Kaffirs, we must note the kraal as the typical village, with its cattle pen **The Kaffir** in the centre, surrounded by a rampart of **kraal.** bushes, and its several rows of conical dwellings, made of poles with interlaced wickerwork, plastered with clay or cowdung, and thatched with straw. They do not exceed seven feet high, and vary from about ten to twenty feet in diameter, in which it may be that thirty persons are accommodated. Rush mats form the usual bedding.

The Kaffirs who have not endeavoured to adopt European style, wear only the kaross of ox or antelope hide, thrown over the shoulders, and hanging down **Clothing.** to the calves. The women also wear an apron decked with beads, or a short petticoat, and many cover the bosom with a piece of dressed skin. The men wear a girdle to which they attach a bag containing their small valuables, a tobacco pouch, etc. Both sexes wear as many beads, necklaces, bracelets, etc., as they can obtain, with anklets and armlets of brass and ivory. Teeth of wild animals furnish necklaces to the chiefs. Not unfrequently they shave their hair, all but a tuft on the top of the head. Large strings of beads **Ornaments.** may be worn through the ear lobe, or a porcupine or bird quill; while sometimes the perforation is stretched till it will receive something enormous. The men usually wear no head-dress, but sometimes have a leather band on the forehead and a copper frontlet with strings of variously coloured beads. Women in some cases wrap a strip of antelope's skin round their head in turban fashion, decked with bead tassels and metal rings. Tattooing is not infrequent, in the form of lines or rows of dots. Oil or grease of some kind is plentifully used to besmear the body, and this is often mixed with ochre to adorn the women's face. Boys and girls wear nothing in youth.

The Kaffirs usually feed on a vegetable diet, such as sorghum and maize cakes, and sour milk. The killing

of an ox is a rare event, celebrated by a feast. Wild
honey is an article of diet; but salt is disliked.

Food. Hospitality is very general, an ox for a feast
being usually given to visitors.

The essentially pastoral occupation of the Kaffirs would
scarcely be imagined from their warlike achievements;
Herding and but they have vast herds of cattle, with which
hunting. they wander from place to place as pasturage
varies; and the men for the most part look after the
herds and the dairy work, women being excluded. Indeed, the Kaffirs have attained high skill in their herding,
driving their cattle by means of trained leaders, and using
peculiar clubs, called knob-kerries, to keep them in order.
The swiftest oxen are trained for riding. The milk of
the cows is put into a common bag of skin, and left till
it is sour and curdled, before it is served out at meals.
Pastoral work, however, does not prevent the Kaffirs from
keen enjoyment of hunting, and they have a large choice
of game. Long spears, which they can throw with great
precision, are their principal weapons. Ambushes, circular
driving to a centre, snares, and pitfalls are largely employed.

The Kaffir women are for the most part menial drudges;
and it is a general subject of complaint, that in Natal
Condition and elsewhere the man lives in idleness on the
of women. profits or produce of his wives' labour. It is
remarkable, however, with what a light heart they appear to endure their subjection; yet there are unending
jealousies between different wives, becoming more bitter
as the position of the family is higher. They are open to
flattery, and coquetry is quite in their line; but in many
tribes their conduct is modest and sensible. Wives are

Marriage. bought for so many head of cattle, the price
sometimes being assessed by the general assembly. There is often a good deal of examination and
criticism of intended brides by the bridegroom's relatives,
a practice not quite unknown in civilised countries. The
bride's dancing,—while the bridegroom sits idly by,—is
not unfrequently a great feature of the pre-nuptial ceremonies, which are unaccompanied by religious rites.

Divorces are rare, but punishment for unfaithfulness is severe; a fine of cattle from a male offender will atone for seduction.

New-born children are rubbed over with powdered shell-lime mixed with water. Children are suckled two years at least, and are treated well, being carried over the shoulder or on the back of the **Children.** mother. The breasts are usually so lengthened that they can either be passed under the arm or over the shoulder, and so suckled. Circumcision is generally performed when boys are full grown, at which time a series of

KAFFIR BENGUERA CUSTOM.

arduous exercises, including severe beatings, is undergone by the youths. This is called the *benguera*. They are then painted with several layers of white clay mixed with blood and water, and invested with the kaross and manly weapons. There is much feasting, dancing, and singing at these times.

Tribes in a pastoral and hunting state, and much occupied with war, have seldom made much progress in industrial arts. Till lately they manufactured **Manufac-** their own rude tools and weapons; but even **tures.** this art will be lost with the advent of foreign traders. They neither spin nor weave. The women make good mats and baskets of grass and rushes. Their rude pottery is sun-dried; but they make very large pots and pans in this way. Calf and sheep skins are sewn together for milk-bags; but the milk is first received into pails. Hides are dressed by the men, the skin being stretched, scraped, rubbed with aloe-leaves, and greased with fat, of course with various intervals of exposure to the sun. Their snuff-boxes are very ingeniously made on small models of animals, which are afterwards broken up through a hole, which afterwards serves as the opening of the box, and is closed by a carved stopper. Wooden spoons and bowls are also among their manufactures, as well as pipes with polished and carved bowls.

CETEWAYO.

The Kaffirs have more aptitude for trade than for manufacture. Their cattle serve as the principal articles of barter, but beads and metal of various kinds circulate largely; of course coins are superseding primitive modes of exchange.

As to morals, very varied opinions are given of the Kaffirs. Some find them **Morals and intellect.** all that is evil; others pronounce them good-hearted, independent, hospitable, and sociable, with a keen sense of justice. No doubt they are vain, and easily become arrogant when prosperous. Flattery is meat and drink to the chiefs; insults are like poison to them; and it is not always easy to discover what will be regarded as an insult. They are, however, very revengeful, and capable of great cruelty; yet among themselves they have been known to be very helpful, sympathetic, and considerate. But it must be confessed that in most respects they are intellectually children. Few of them, before the advent of Europeans, had any notion of number beyond ten; nor was their reckoning of time much more advanced; and it is difficult to get from them an idea of the lapse of past time or their own age. However, they were acquainted with some useful medicines, using several roots as stimulants, euphorbia juices for blistering, and aloes for various purposes.

Singing and dancing are their great amusements, often carried on through the night with great boisterousness and wild gestures, sometimes so violent as to produce complete exhaustion. The accom- **Amusements.** panying music is of a very monotonous and unmelodious description, with ceaseless repetitions of the same words. A sort of Jew's harp is their chief instrument.

Government by the chiefs and "kings" is usually despotic, but there is considerable deference to old-established custom. Succession is nominally here- **Government.** ditary in males, but usually the son of the chief wife is selected to succeed; or even hereditary succession may be disregarded if general opinion or some powerful reason suggests one outside the ruling family. The people pay an annual tax of cattle; and the chief may claim portions of every animal, all elephants' tusks, panthers' skins, and other desirable objects. When it is added that the subjects' labour is understood to be absolutely at the chiefs' disposal, it is evident that the ruler has an enviable supremacy. The chief is assisted by subordinate chiefs, or a council of elders, in deciding important cases. The death penalty is frequent, although, when it is more convenient, a fine in cattle is taken. Witchcraft, desertion of the tribe, and murder of a chief or a parent, are visited by the death-penalty.

The Kaffirs cannot be described as having in their uncivilised state any truly religious ideas, for they did not believe in a Supreme Being, nor had they **Superstitions.** any form of worship; but they had a great number of superstitious observances. All kinds of diseases or calamities were attributed to witchcraft or to certain evil agencies. Partaking of firstfruits, rain-making, various feats of magic, etc., are among their important

KAFFIRS TRADING.

functions, in which the chief usually takes the lead, but

in which a special body,—who may be entitled sorcerers rather than priests,—are engaged. These people also practise medicine, and counteract the evil spirits or powers who are supposed to cause diseases. The most extraordinary feats are supposed to be performed by these sorcerers, such as the extraction of a snake, a turtle, or a lizard from the bodies of the sufferers. It is always easy for the sorcerer, if unsuccessful, to allege that the evil spirit was too powerful. At times a sorceress is the acting agent, and sometimes pretends to discover the source of evil in some unlucky man, who is forthwith tortured to death and his property confiscated.

The Gaikas and Galeikas are the most prominent members of the Amakhosa Kaffirs, occupying plains bounded on the north by the Winterberg Mountains, **The** affording plenty of pasture and game. They **Amakhosa.** are tall and well-developed, of light chocolate complexion, with woolly hair, full lips, and white teeth, and graceful in movements. Their moral character is not quite so good as their figure; and cruelty and plunder are frequent among them. They are unkind to the sick and infirm, and exceedingly superstitious. Still they are very hospitable. They do a good deal of agriculture, in which the women have the greatest share, growing sorghum, maize, tobacco, and pumpkins.

The Basutos are a Kaffir people south-east of the Transvaal, but whose original location was north of the Blue Mountains. They are now under British protection. They are not very different from the Bechuanas of **The Basutos.** Central South Africa, several tribes or nations **The** of whom have recently been placed under **Bechuanas.** British rule or protection. The tribes take their name for the most part from notable animals, as elephants, crocodiles, fish, monkeys, etc. As they are not essentially different from the rest of the Kaffirs, we may select some of their more remarkable superstitions and practices for notice. While their beliefs can hardly be dignified with the name of religion, they invoke the souls of their renowned chiefs (*barimo*) when any distress or famine overtakes the tribe. They have in these circumstances been known to cut themselves with small knives, lie down in ashes, and cry aloud most bitterly. Groans and lugubrious songs, with solemn dances, vary the cere-monies, which may be continued day and night. Then

Superstitions. they go through their hunting haunts once more to examine their traps and snares. Some of them consider that things have grown of themselves; but while not regarding any powerful benevolent being, they attribute evils and calamities to an evil agency which they name *moleino*, whose action can be antagonised by charms and by their sorcerers. To secure a good harvest, they burn certain plants and certain parts of animals. Some tribes in past times have burnt human victims for this purpose.

The name of *lin-yaka* is applied to the professional rain-makers, sorcerers, and **The linyakas.** medicine men. A gift of an ox secures admission to the pro-fession, followed by initiation, called "teaching to dig,"

ZULU KAFFIRS.

because the sources of medicines and charms are pointed out in the forests. They wear a baboon skin, and in their huts they sit on a hyena skin. "Many of them," says Dr. Holub, "wear round their necks whole strings of the bones of different mammals, birds, and reptiles, and all, without exception, are provided with four little pegs,—generally made of ivory but sometimes of horn, and branded over with figures,—which are thrown like dice," being used in their pretended investigations. These pegs are called *dolos;* and, in addition to amulets of all kinds of bones and pieces of skin, these dolos play an important part, being brought into play " to find out the whereabouts of stolen goods or the retreat of a fugitive, as well as to exorcise obnoxious men and beasts; they are considered capable of charming away an enemy and of averting mischief, certain formulæ generally being recited whenever they are employed." Some of these linyakas, how- *The moloi.* ever, are hateu, and termed " moloi," having been known to act from revenge, or with an unfavourable effect. All kinds of impossible evils and powers are attributed to them; they are said to dig up corpses and kill new-born infants, to use parts of their bodies in their incantations. But it may be considered that these moloi are the instruments or the cloak for private revenge. They also claim the power of warding off rain and thwarting the efforts of the regular rain-makers.

Many of these superstitions are gradually dying under the influence of the missionaries, but some of them die hard; some of the Bechuana kings, after their *Influence of* conversion, have attempted to carry on their *Christianity.* old rain-making practices. Some successful schools have been established among them, and not a few of the population are now able to read translations of the Bible into their own languages; and native teachers and preachers of tried integrity have been trained among them. Altogether, it may be expected that in time these South African natives may become to Europeans something like the native races of India became to the Aryan invaders, without so many of the caste differences which the Aryans made into a religion in India, and which have *Future of* been too much in fashion in South Africa. *the natives.* They have not to fear extinction, if they become useful to the superior races; and it will be great folly if the white races do not adopt regulations for protecting and preserving a useful population of workers, rather than consign them to the fate which is overtaking the red man in America and the Maori of New Zealand.

CHAPTER IX.
South Tropical Africans.

The Damaras—Physical type—Character—Treatment of sick and infirm—
Superstitions—The Ovampos—Other Bantu tribes—Handicrafts—Burial
customs—Warlike character—The Wanyamuesi—The Manyema—Natives
of Kizambala—Natives of Rubunga—The Wayanzi—People of Zanzibar
—Mixture of races—The slave trade—The Suaheli—The Wanyika—The
Masai and Wakwafi—Military organisation—The recent scramble for
Africa—French possessions—German sphere of influence—The Congo
Free State — Portuguese
territory — Loango, Ka-
benda, Kakongo — The
Bunda tribes—Character
of Angolese negroes—A
state reception—Slavery
and trade—Market scene
at Loanda — Costume —
European residents —
Kingdom of Congo —
Other Bantu kingdoms.

DAMARA CHIEF'S TOMB.

178

TRAVELLING northward from the Cape districts, we meet with a succession of tribes, some of which are more allied to the Kaffirs, others to the Equatorial negroes. The Damaras and Ovampos were both made known largely by

Mr. Francis Galton ("Narrative of an Explorer in Tropical South Africa," 1853). The Damaras of the Plain are true Bantu, while the Hill Damaras are Hottentots, who have been dispossessed of the plains by the former. The Plain Damaras, who call themselves Ovaherero, are tall, handsome and well-proportioned; and the women when young are good-looking, with small hands and feet, Physical but as they grow older they become ugly and type. repulsive. Various species of mimosa, with palms, are the chief vegetation; and the vast desert country is often devastated by sand-storms. The conical huts of the Damaras, which in several respects resemble those of the Kaffirs, are often covered with ox-hides. Beds are made

DAMARA HUTS.

of leafy mimosa branches covered with skins. In dress the Damaras have a general resemblance to the Kaffirs. They knock out the two lower incisors, and file a triangular space between the two upper front teeth. They possess an immense number of cattle and sheep, which they guard by means of dogs.

The Damaras are not very advanced intellectually or morally, and are correspondingly suspicious and addicted to plunder and begging. They can count but little, and

do not know their own ages. It is said that they be-
Character. lieved the sun which rises in the morning is
quite different from that which set on the
previous evening. Polygamy flourishes among them, and
divorce is frequent and unceremonious; the wives, according to Mr. Galton, have rather the upper hand, being very
useful to the men, doing most of the household work, and

DAMARA SMOKING PARTY.

even building and plastering the hut, and carrying the
baggage when a removal takes place. Brotherly kindness
does not flourish greatly among them, for it is said very
Treatment few Damaras die a natural death. A sick per-
of sick and son, says Mr. Galton, meets with no compassion;
infirm. he is pushed out of his hut into the cold; his
relatives do all they can to hasten his death, and when he

appears to be dying, they suffocate him by heaping ox-hides over him. After death the body is sewn up in an old ox-hide in a sitting posture, and buried in a hole dug for it, the face being turned towards the north. The relatives, or those who are present, jump backwards and forwards over the grave to prevent disease from rising out of it. A person of importance, or a chief, is however mourned for and buried with lamentation and various ceremonies.

The superstitions of the Damaras are very numerous. Some eat no mutton, others will eat no beef from cattle with particular kinds of spots. Hyena dung is regarded as a **Superstitions.** great "medicine," and is used to rub the mouth and fore-head of a patient. Greasing with the fat of some particular animal is believed to be of much virtue. Fire is maintained by the care of the chief's daughter; and should it by chance be extin-

SOUTH AFRICAN HEADDRESSES.

guished, a great ceremony and much sacrificing of cattle are necessary when it is rekindled. They have no definite religious ideas; and it is even doubtful if they think of evil agencies in nature. They have a story of the origin of all living things from a tree.

The Ovampos are of a very different type. Mr. Galton at once perceived the contrast on seeing them for the first time. They are fine, ugly, bony men with **The Ovampos.** strongly-marked features, very dark in complexion and with woolly hair, sometimes completely shaved. They have no towns, dwelling in distant farm-homesteads, which are very complex structures, especially those of the chiefs, being really a collection of houses wherein families of several generations, together with slaves, are accommodated; but all the buildings are of small height, although the outer close palisading is as high as they can make it. Individual houses are absurdly small: only about five and a half feet across and three feet high, with a conical thatched roof; the door is but two feet high and one and a half broad; each hut is occupied by an entire family. Sorghum and millet with milk are the staple foods, oxen being only killed on festival occasions; but they eat the flesh of almost every animal. They drink a beer fermented from sorghum.

WOMAN OF ZAMBESI.

The Ovampos wear less clothing than the Kaffirs; aprons of dressed skin before and behind being the principal garments. Ear-rings of beads or shells, portions of ostrich egg-shell, bead necklaces, etc., are worn. The middle lower incisors are chipped or filed. In many respects the Ovampos resemble the Kaffirs, and it is probable that they must be classed among the Bantu.

The Bantu tribes of East Africa include probably the relatives of the Southern Bantu, North of the Zambesi and East of Lake Nyassa, hence very similar customs are found among them. Their moral state is Other Bantu very rudimentary, and they are fickle, venal, and tribes. idle, gay and cunning. Many of them have cuts or tattoo marks on the body, some being high continuous ridges. Like so many of the Kaffir tribes, they use no salt, or only use it on rare occasions. Their agriculture is varied, including many forms of pulse, sweet potatoes, and manioc, as well as cereals. Tobacco and cotton are among their crops. They have few domestic cattle, but kill many wild animals. They are said to have learnt from the Portuguese who hold the Mozambique coast to smelt iron ore and make agricultural imple- Handicrafts. ments. They can also weave reed mats, and make bamboo baskets so skilfully that they are watertight. They make thread out of bark fibre, and make fishing-nets of it, and can even spin cotton into yarn and make a coarse kind of cloth. They cross their rivers in canoes of bark sewn together with cords.

Polygamy is customary among them ; and women are regularly sold by their parents, or even offered to strangers by their husbands. The women do all the work Burial that can be got out of them ; only the men customs. build the huts. The burial of chiefs is a time of great feasting and licence. The corpse is kept enveloped in cloth and allowed to putrefy, and several months elapse before burial. One of the strange customs supposed to show reverence to the dead, is indiscriminate robbing and beating of people. The usual loud lamentations and beatings of drums attend the funeral. His favourite weapons are buried with the chief, and a great quantity of palm wine is poured out. Not so long ago it was the custom to bury the chief's wives with him. Many offer-ings of food and drink are made during the prolonged ceremonies, which last eight days. The Makuas or Makoas, North-east of the Shiré, bury their dead near their houses, placing the body upright and naked in a grave. Their shrieking is of a horrible description, and they cut off their hair in token of mourning.

The chiefs hold their position mainly by virtue of

warlike prowess, and are continually involved in strife,
Warlike character. in which they use poisoned arrows, spears, hatchets, and knives. They show great courage,

HEAD MEN IN THE ROVUMA DISTRICT, EAST AFRICA.   THE MAN ON THE RIGHT IS A MAVIA.
(*From a Photograph lent by Dr. Beddoe, F.R.S.*)

attacking their enemies in a body without organization, and with wild war-cries. The Makuas are especially obstinate in their warfare, fighting to the death, and

sacrificing their prisoners, whose flesh they eat raw. They
are recognised by having a crescent tattooed on their
foreheads. They all wear a lip-ring and file their teeth
sharp. Some missionary efforts among them appear to
give promise of good results.

The Manganjas are a numerous people inhabiting the
uplands around the Valley of the Shiré. The women
almost universally wear the *pelele*, a shell or ring extending the upper lip enormously forward. On the Rovuma
river it is worn even by the men. As is so usual among
African tribes, they are great believers in the poison
ordeal.

The shores of Lake Nyassa are thickly peopled, all the
people being tattooed from head to foot with figures
which specially mark the tribe. The Matumboka, who
live to the west of the lake, produce little wart-like eleva-
tions on the face, giving a very repulsive appearance to
the women.

It is scarcely as yet possible to take a general view of
the people of this vast region, except to say that they are
for the most part more allied in race, and far more in
language, to the Kaffirs, than to the Soudanese Negroes.
We must content ourselves for the most part with following the descriptions of the more notable ex- The
plorers. Cameron ("Across Africa") thus de- **Wanyamuesi.**
scribes the natives of Wanyamuesi, north-east of Ugogo.
Their distinguishing tribal marks are "a tattooed line
down the centre of the forehead and on each temple; the
two upper front teeth are chipped so as to show a chevron-
shaped gap; and a small triangular piece of hippopotamus
ivory or of shell, ground down white and polished, is hung
round the neck. Their ornaments consist principally of
beads and brass and iron wire. Chiefs and headmen
wear enormous cylindrical bracelets of ivory, extending
from wrist to elbow, which are used also as signals in
warfare. The noise occasioned by striking them together
is heard at a long distance, and is used by the chiefs as
a call for their men to rally round them. The men
usually shave the crown of the head, and wear their hair
twisted into innumerable small strings."

Of the Manyema, north-west of Lake Tanganyika, Stanley says ("Through the Dark Continent"): "Their

The Manyema. arms are a short sword, scabbarded with wood, to which are hung small brass and iron bells, and a light, beautifully balanced spear. Their shields were veritable wooden doors. Their dress consisted of a narrow apron of antelope skin or finely made grass-cloth. They wore knobs, cones, and patches of mud attached to their beards, back hair, and behind the ears. At Kizambala, the natives had horns and cones of mud on the tops of their heads. Others, more ambi-

Natives of Kizambala. tious, covered the entire head with a crown of mud. The women, blessed with an abundance of hair, manufactured it with a stiffening of light cane into a bonnet-shaped head-dress, allowing the back hair to flow down to the waist in masses of ringlets. They seemed to do all the work of life, for at all hours they might be seen, with their large wicker baskets behind them, setting out for the rivers or creeks to catch fish, or returning with their fuel baskets strapped on across their foreheads. Their villages consist of one or more broad streets from 100 to 150 feet wide, flanked by low, square huts arranged in tolerably

MANYEMA GIRL.

straight lines, and generally situated on swells of land, to secure rapid drainage. At the end of one of these streets is the council and gossip-house, overlooking the length of the avenue. In the centre is a platform, of tamped clay, with a heavy tree-trunk sunk into it, and in the wood have been scooped out a number of troughs, so that several women may pound grain at once. The houses are separated into two or more apartments; and on account of the compact nature of the clay and tamped floor are easily kept clean. The roofs are shiny with the reek of smoke, as though they had been painted with coal-tar. The household chattels or furniture are limited to food-baskets, earthenware pots, an assortment of wicker-work dishes, the family shield, spears, knives, swords, and tools, and the fish-baskets lying outside. They are tolerably hospitable, and permit strangers the free use of their dwellings. The bananas and plantains are very luxuriant, while the Guinea palms supply the people with oil and wine; the forests give them fuel, the rivers fish, and the gardens cassava, ground-nuts, and Indian corn. The chiefs enact strict laws, and though possessed of but little actual power,

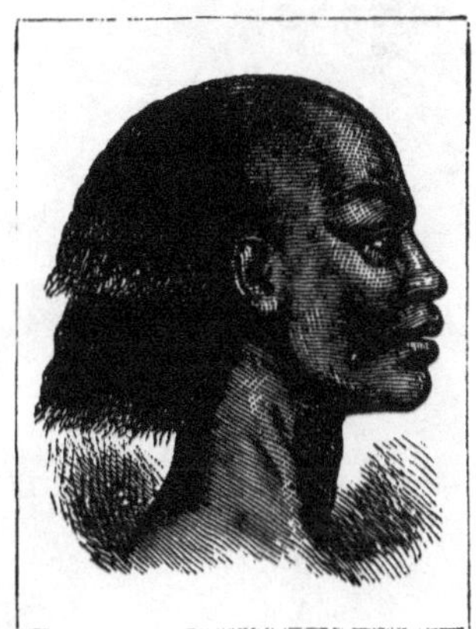

ADULT AND YOUTH OF EAST MANYEMA.

either of wealth or retinue, exact the utmost deference, and are exceedingly ceremonious, being always followed by a drummer, who taps his drum with masterly skill."

At Rubunga, about the most northerly point reached by the Congo, the natives dress their hair in tufts on the back of the head, fastened with iron hair-pins. **Natives of Rubunga.** "Tattooing is carried to excess, every portion of the skin bearing punctured marks, from the roots of the hair down to the knees. Their breasts are like hieroglyphic parchment charts, marked with raised figures, ledges, squares, circles, wavy lines, tuberose knots, rosettes,

VILLAGE IN SOUTH-EAST MANYEMA.

and every conceivable design. No colouring substance
had been introduced into these incisions and punctures;
the cuticle had simply been tortured and irritated by the
injection of some irritants or air. Indeed, some of the
glossy tubercles, which contained air, were as large as
hens' eggs. As many as six thin ledges marked the foreheads from temple to temple, as many ran down each
cheek, while from lower eyelid to base of septum curved
wavy lines, the chin showed rosettes, the neck seemed
goitrous with the large
vesicular protuber-
ances, while the front
parts of their bodies
afforded broad fields
upon which the native
artist had displayed the
exuberant fertility of
his genius." Conse-
quently these people
appear hideously de-
formed. Their neck-
laces consist of human,
gorilla, and crocodile
teeth, so numerous as
to almost cover the
neck. Many of these
Central Africans ce-
ment friendship by
performing the rite of
blood-brotherhood, be-
fore or after an ex-

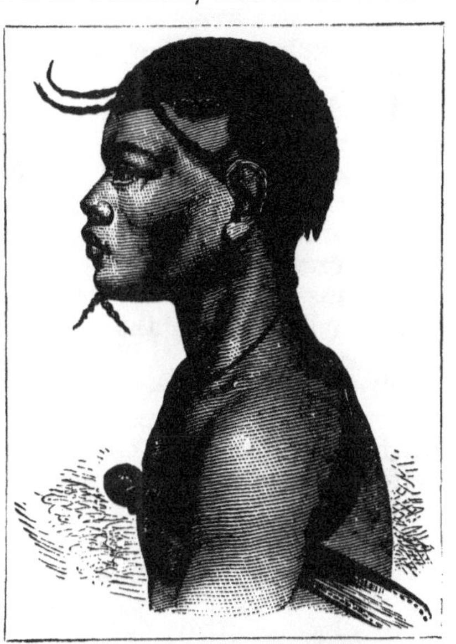

SON OF A CHIEF, CHUMBIRI.

change of gifts. The Rubunga people were so eager and
vigorous about it that Mr. Stanley thought the proceeding very cannibalistic. After an incision was made in
each arm, the two " brothers " bent their heads, and the
native sucked with the greatest fervour and gusto.

At Chumbiri, a good way further to the south-west, the
(Wayanzi) women wore large brass collars, from two to
three inches in diameter, some weighing thirty
pounds, soldered permanently round the neck, **The Wayanzi.**

in addition to several pounds of brass wire for arm and leg ornaments. The warriors and young men wore their hair in four separate plaits, two of which overhung the forehead. Two lines are very generally tattooed on the forehead. The Babwende, still lower down, have a curious habit. While visiting Stanley with gifts, and having seated themselves for a chat, they suddenly began grinding their teeth, as though in a mad rage.

We must reluctantly restrict our accounts of the African tribes, and not even mention many tribes described by various explorers. They are, however, as yet but little known scientifically. When they are more thoroughly compared together, they will be found to fall into a few important groups, whose customs can be classified and compared. Till then, it is wearisome and bewildering to read of the vast numbers of savage tribes already made known, unless in the pages of some great explorer like Livingstone or Stanley.

We must briefly refer to the people of the Zanzibar district, where the Mahometans are once more found in **People of** full force. The islands of Zanzibar, Pemba, **Zanzibar.** and Mafia, with a portion of adjacent coast, are pretty well all that is now left to the Sultan of Zanzibar, who formerly swayed the whole Suaheli coast. But this itself was only a modern arrangement, for not a quarter of a century ago this tract belonged to the Imam of Muscat (South-east Arabia). On the death of a recent imam, however, his territory was divided between his two sons. Seyyid Bargash, a Wahabee, became Sultan of Zanzibar in 1870; his brother, Seyyid Khalifah, succeeded him early in 1888. Here the population has be- **Mixture of** come a somewhat distinct type, owing to the **races.** large intermixture of Arabs for many generations with the Bantu Suaheli; indeed, so strong is the influence of the Arab blood, that the people in general call themselves Arabs, and are zealous, sometimes fanatical, Mahometans. The town of Zanzibar has a very mixed and crowded population, including, besides Arabs and Suaheli, many Malagasy, Hindus, Lascars, and Negro slaves. The town is a fine one, with houses of white stone. The Hindus are of many tribes and castes, and carry on the greater part of the trade, both import and retail; but few of them settle permanently; they nearly all return home when they have made enough money. The slave trade, though nominally

The slave trade.

THE LATE SULTAN OF ZANZIBAR.

suppressed in all these regions, still continues only too actively, though in a more secret fashion than formerly. It will require some generations at least before it can be extinguished, for the spirit of slavery is deeply ingrained in the Africans themselves. So many tribes are eager to enslave others, or to sell their own relatives for money or valued articles, that the great demand from Persia, Arabia, etc., will long create a supply. The horrors of the slave capture and the slave march are, however, far worse than those of actual slavery, and yearly destroy very many thousands of victims. Nothing but the most determined efforts of civilised powers will, however, suffice to put a stop to African slavery; and it is to be feared that vast numbers of Africans will do no work at all, unless under compulsion.

The Suaheli are usually robust and well-formed, of a chocolate-brown complexion, with short, woolly, crisp hair and scanty beard. They have prominent lips and jaws, and somewhat flat noses. The Arab style of dress is, by those well-to-do, generally adopted. Long white tunics, covering a coloured vest, turbans, and sandals are worn. The women usually wear a short-sleeved silk or cotton gown, and the face is veiled, often with black silk; a blue or black skirt is worn over the gown.

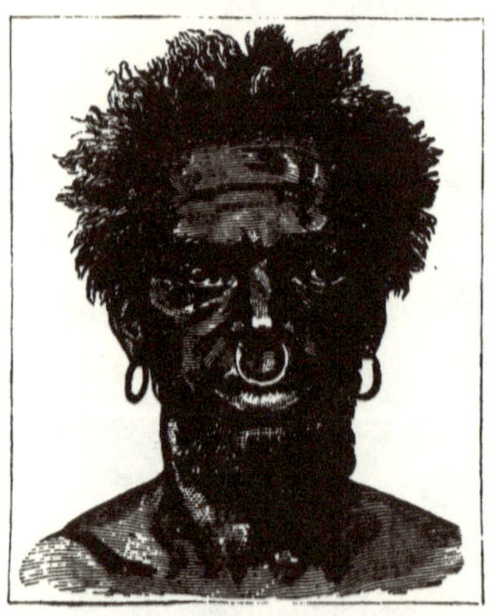

SUAHELI.

Their eyebrows are blackened with soot, and their finger nails reddened with henna. The poorer men have a simple short kilt, the women wrap a cotton cloth round their body below the shoulders. While hospitable and friendly to strangers, they are often extremely cunning, selfish, and mendacious. They are often very adept in concealing their thoughts, and have much assurance and self-esteem. They are very conservative, and not easily moved out of customary paths, often drink to excess, and have little or no regard to chastity. Still they make strong attachments, and can be made into faithful servants by those posesssed of the right genius. Agriculture is largely followed, and domestic cattle are numerous. The Suaheli language is one of the Bantu languages, and has spread very widely on the coast, and in the interior of Eastern Africa.

The Wanyika are a people further inland, between 3° and 5° south. They are an impudent warlike people—some, however, being very cowardly; but their **The** character in general is painted in very dark **Wanyika.** colours. They are still very primitive, wearing round their waist only a dressed skin or a piece of native cotton or bark-cloth ; on their legs they wear pieces of hairy ox hide. They shave the hair off their forehead, and the rest is trained and stiffened with fat into screw-like tufts, into which an ostrich or other feather is stuck. They are very fluent talkers, and very fond of pleasure, having many riotous festivals. The women do nearly all the work, and the men have many wives, who are bought. The son of a Wanyika chief is not recognised as adult until he has killed a man, no matter whom. The dead are buried in deep graves, with the head turned towards the south-west. The ghosts of the dead are believed to haunt the neighbourhood of the chief town of the tribe, where huts are built for them, and offerings made to them. They are very superstitious, and believe in beings called *mulungu*, who are both good and evil, and may represent the powers of nature. All diseases are believed to be caused by them, and consequently a medicine-man is called in to exorcise the evil spirit. Rain-makers are devoutly believed in.

The Masai and the Wakwafi of the Kilima-njaro region are said to show relationship to the Hamitic peoples, but this can hardly be settled yet. They have pro- **The Masai** jecting jaws and high cheek-bones, but their **and** hair is straight. They are of a very ferocious **Wakwafi.** type, and are continually at war with one another ; but all foreigners are hateful to them. They show great courage, but defer much to their seniors. They have no settled abodes, but camp in suitable places for a longer or shorter time, forming regular towns with tent-like huts

covered with hides and grass. The whole town is surrounded by a thorn-like hedge and a ditch, and sentinels
are always on guard. They are largely pastoral, having
heads of cattle, sheep, and goats. Their diet is chiefly
animal, and they make butter and eat honey.

Women are in a very subordinate position among these

MASAI MARRIED WOMAN.

people. They are sometimes tortured or mutilated; girls
are fattened for marriage. Polygamy is common, wives
being bought for a certain number of cattle.

The Masai claim exclusive ownership of the surrounding plains and wilderness, and are very difficult to deal
Military with, owing to their warlike organisation.
organisation. Their armies number several thousand men.

and they usually try to completely surround their enemy.
They maintain a very severe discipline, a coward being
cut to pieces before the eyes of the rest. They often
make predatory expeditions, and lay waste the whole
country, not taking prisoners, but killing men and women
in cold blood. They have thick clubs which they can
throw a hundred feet with great precision, often dashing
out the brains of an enemy. They have an idea of the
sky, or rain (called Eugai), as a great power, which they
suppose dwells on Kilima-njaro; but they invoke an
ancestral hero to intercede with Eugai. The medicine-
man and sorcerer are as powerful among them as among
most other African tribes.

It would be fruitless to attempt as yet to define precisely
the possessions of various European powers in the regions
we have been describing. Vast tracts have *The recent
scramble for Africa.* been claimed by or assigned to the various
powers by agreement among themselves, and
too often without taking much account of the natives;
but these so-called protectorates, or "spheres of influence,"
are in many cases very unreal at present, and amount to
little but the occupation of portions of coast line and of
river bank, and the assertion of a certain amount of
authority over the natives when they threaten to become
troublesome to traders. Colonisation in the true sense
scarcely exists, and it is doubtful whether it can ever be
thoroughly carried out. France has almost all *French
possessions.* the West Coast, from Campo river (2° 20′ N.)
down to the Loango river, about 5° S., including the
Gaboon and the Ogoway rivers, and a large part of the
north-west bank of the Congo. Germany has *German
sphere of influence.* the coast north of this French territory, including the Cameroons district, and south of
the Portuguese territory, from Cape Frio to the Orange
River (excepting the small British settlement of Walfisch
Bay), and claims some influence as far as 20° east latitude,
thus including Damaraland and Great Namaqualand.
Germany has also obtained the large region between
Mount Kilima-njaro and the river Rovuma, oppositethe
middle of Lake Nyassa.

ON THE WAR PATH IN MASAI LAND.

The Congo Free State, under the auspices of the King of the Belgians, and of Mr. H. M. Stanley, possesses a tract on the north bank of the Congo from its *The Congo Free State.* mouth to Manyanga, where the French come in, and claim this bank as far as the mouth of the Likona. Thence the Congo State claims rights as far as 4° N. and 30° E., and south to Lake Bangweolo (12° S.), and west to 24° E., reaching northward to 6° S. and westwards to the south bank of the Congo at Nokki. The estimated area is over a million square miles, which Mr. Stanley imagines to contain twenty-seven millions of people.

The Portuguese colonies in South Africa are extensive, partly of long standing, partly of recent acquisition. They include, on the West Coast, in the former class, *Portuguese territory.* stations north of the Congo (Cabenda and Loango), the southern mouth of that river up to Nokki, with all the intervening territory to Ambriz ; while Angola, Benguela, and Mossamedes, extending down to the German line at Cape Frio, are old settlements. On the East Coast, Portugal has held Mozambique and Sofala since the end of the fifteenth century, and is now allowed to rule from near Cape Delgado to Delagoa Bay ; only a small part of this immense territory is really held. Portugal, however, now claims a belt of land extending right across Africa between her eastern and western colonies.

In addition to Bechuanaland, British influence has lately been asserted over the territory north of the German cession from Zanzibar, extending across the *British power.* equatorial region, and to Lake Victoria Nyanza. Thus the scramble for Africa has left Great Britain in possession of the most fertile and habitable portions of South Africa, with by far the most advanced settlements, and considerably more than one-third of the total external trade of the continent. France has about one quarter of the external trade. It is to be hoped that, without further quarrelling, all parties will set to work to make the best possible use of their "spheres of influence," and realize that the course which is best for the interests and welfare of the natives will in the long run be best for European traders.

In the territory recognised as Portuguese, the coast kingdoms of Loango, Kabenda, and Kakongo, north of the Congo, were formerly subject to the king of the native state of Congo. Here the fetish priests are still supreme, really electing the

Loango, Kabenda, Kakongo.

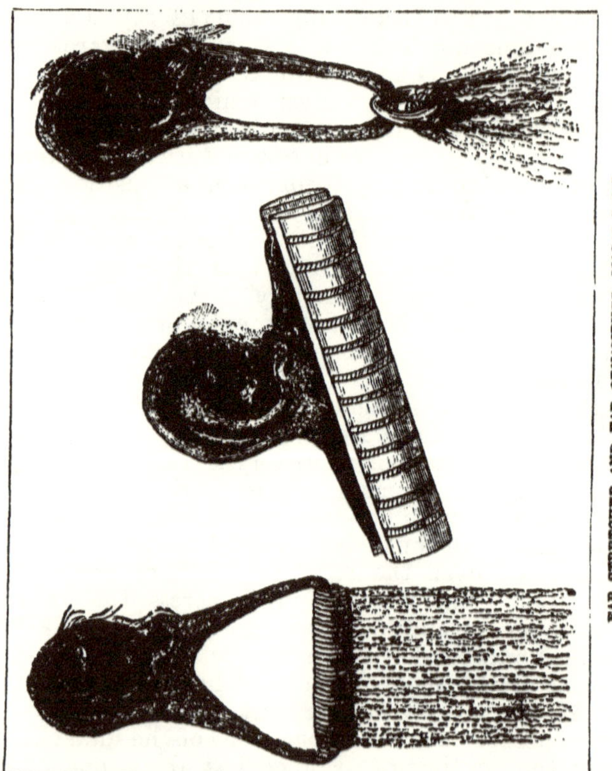

kings, and keeping them under strict control by the rites they enforce and the very numerous things they forbid them to do or see. In some cases these restrictions are so irksome that no native can for years be induced to accept the throne; then the coffin of the dead king is kept unburied, and the fetish priests rule meanwhile. Their tyrannical influence over the people is almost unbounded. The natives are rather undersized and not so muscular as many negroes, but have considerable skill in the arts, some being excellent weavers and making silk-like fabrics out of little but bast and straw.

Immediately south of the Congo the tribes are in a more primitive condition than in Angola proper; but the men wear a waistcloth fastened with a bit of **The Bunda** red baize, and the women are still more cov- **tribes.** ered. The Mussurongo are a piratical tribe near the mouth of the river on both sides, who shave their heads, or cut the hair short, or into peculiar patterns. They belong to a division of Bantu known as the Bunda group, also including the people of Loango. All these retain some of the education and Christian ideas spread among them by Portuguese missionaries two centuries ago; but some of the tribes under Portuguese rule are among the most degraded of Africans, very ugly, wild, savage, and suspicious.

Mr. Monteiro, in his " Angola and the River Congo," gives a very unfavourable picture of the negroes in that region. He regards the development of the **Character of** miasma-proof negro as coincident with an arrest **Angolese** of development of the intellect. He has never **negroes.** in many years seen a negro show the least tenderness towards a negress, or kiss or caress one. Their passions are purely of an animal description, and jealousy scarcely exists, unfaithfulness in a wife being punishable by fining the paramour. Mothers are rarely seen fondling or playing with their babies. They all delight in witnessing an animal tortured; and a negro may be thrashed to within an inch of his life and show no malice or vindictiveness afterwards. Similarly, no benefit is a subject of gratitude, though he may express pleasure at obtaining something without effort. Even among those who have accepted the white man's idea of a Creator, there remains the belief that the white man's God is different from that of the black man. The fetish system is still fully in force. There are few great chiefs among these people, every

town having its own chief and council, usually ten or
twelve of the elders, termed Macotas.   The office of chief
or king descends from uncle to nephew or niece, by the
sister's side.   " Every king has a stick of office ; this is
in form like a straight, thick, smooth walking-stick,
generally made of ebony, or of other wood dyed black.
These sticks are always sent with a messenger from the
king, and serve to authenticate the message.   The principal insignia of the king's office is the cap, which is
hereditary.   It resembles a short nightcap, and is made
of fine fibre, generally that of the wild pineapple leaf,
and some are beautifully woven with raised patterns.
The king never wears it in the usual way, but on any
occasion of ceremony it is carried on the head doubled
in four.

" The appearance of some of the kings dressed in their
fine clothes is very ridiculous.   A red or blue baize cloak
Amusing thrown over the shoulders is considered the
royal dress. correct thing, particularly over an old uniform
of any kind, the more gold lace on it the better.   The
old king of Quirillo, on the road to Bembe, was as amusing
a figure as any I have seen.   He always used to appear
in a woman's brightly-coloured chintz gown, with a short
red cloak over his shoulders, and a great brass cavalry
helmet over his head, his black wrinkled face in a broad
grin of satisfaction."

As a specimen of African manners, few occasions are
more typical than the reception of travellers by native
A state kings ; and these are often similar over a wide
reception. tract of country.   The king dresses in his best,
and the meeting takes place in front of the king's abode
or under a great baobab tree.   The servants of the
traveller on the one side and almost the whole of the inhabitants on the other, squat or stand about.   In the
Angola region the traveller's retinue first " clap hands,"
to the king and macotas.   The king in return extends
his left hand horizontally in front of him with the palm
upwards, placing the back of the right hand flat on the
left palm, and waving the projecting fingers quickly in
succession.   The king then addresses one of the macotas,

delivering his welcome to the traveller, who puts forward one of his attendants as interpreter, and the macota delivers to him the king's speech; through him too the traveller returns his compliments, and makes the king suitable presents, including of course a bottle of wine or rum, which the king and his macotas drink ; and the king makes the traveller a small present in return. It is most essential to employ interpreters in this procedure, however well the parties may understand one another's language.

Slavery seems to have been a natural product of negro life in Angola and Benguela; and although the Portuguese till lately maintained it, and recognised it, it does **Slavery and** not appear to have **trade** been of a very harsh description, slaves living in the utmost amity with their masters, and mistresses and slaves working together in the fields. Formerly there were great exportations of slaves from Portuguese West Africa to Brazil, concurrent with the ivory trade, for which slaves were needful as carriers. Many kinds of agriculture and trade have sprung up in late years. The groundnut is largely exported for its

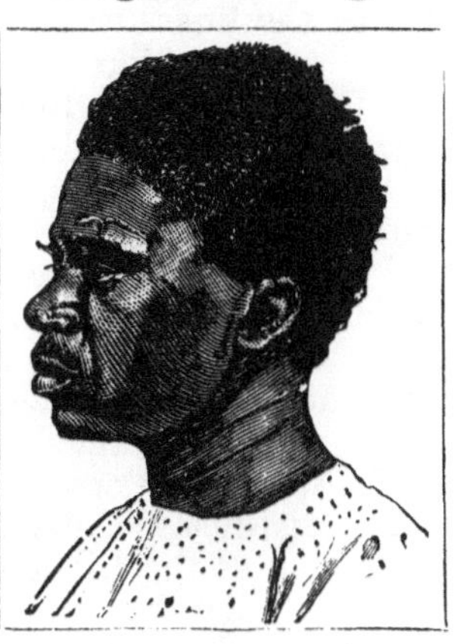

CONGO NEGRO.

oil ; cotton is increasingly grown ; baobab bark fibre, indiarubber, copal gum, etc., are also important products. But for the most part the bad government of Portugal has failed egregiously to develop the resources of the country.

Loanda, or St. Paul de Loanda, is a developing town, with considerable public buildings, good shops and stores, and wide roads and streets. The open market **Market scene** is a scene of great excitement and noise. The **at Loanda.** vendors are mostly women, wearing straw hats with brims almost as large as umbrellas. Here may be seen, according to Monteiro, all kinds of dishes attractive to negroes :

wooden dishes full of small pieces of pork; pots of cooked
beans and palm oil, retailed in large spoonfuls eaten on
the spot; terrible-looking messes of fish, cakes, and pastry,
thickly covered with large flies, jars of Indian-corn beer,
live fowls, ducks, white tomatoes, bananas, and all kinds
of fruits. The women squat on their heels, with their
wares in front; and their babies roll about in the sand and
rubbish, with a swarm of mongrel dogs and lean, long-
snouted pigs quarrelling for stray morsels. Fish is abundant on this coast.

The usual negro dress in Angola is a waistcloth reaching to the knees or ankles, and another thrown over the
shoulders; but an approach to European costume is often made, the chimney-pot hat being
a great object of ambition. The women wear an indigo-
black cotton cloth, tightly folded round the body from
armpits to feet; and another long piece covers the head,
and is crossed over the chest, or hangs loosely down over
the shoulders. Beneath this they usually have a coloured
print, and this alone is worn by the poorer classes. Both
men and women talk aloud to themselves while walking.

Benguela, Mossamedes, and Ambriz are other considerable towns in Portuguese territory. There are some
tribes distinctly differing from the prevailing Bunda
type, such as the Libollo and the Quissama, which tribes
are hereditary enemies. These have hitherto maintained
almost complete independence of the Portuguese. They
are short, very dark, and extremely dirty in their habits.
There are numerous other timid and small-sized tribes,
which appear to be remains of primitive peoples fast
disappearing, some living in caves and fissures in the
hills, and fleeing before visitors.

This great country is inhabited by but a handful of
Europeans, most of whom only look for a return home
when they have made a fortune; and few
indeed are the instances of anything like complete acclimatisation. In Mossamedes alone, in the south
of the Portuguese territory, do the families of Europeans
flourish; and nearly to this point the Boers have extended
their "trekking" from Southern Africa. Brazilian immi-

grants, too, partly of Portuguese blood, are settling here. There are also some Canarese half-breeds from Goa, who occupy positions as priests, teachers, and accountants. Such is the feeble contribution which the European races have made to a country which they have despoiled in three centuries of at least a million of slaves, whose capture and transport probably represents the destruction of three or four millions.

The so-called kingdom of Congo abuts on the Portuguese possessions on the north-east; it has now but a shadow of its former influence. Three hundred **Kingdom of Congo.** years ago, when the Jesuits "converted" it, the king ruled over a large number of subordinate chiefs and territories, and could assemble a large army. The king's power was kept up by his control of the slave and ivory trade, and his receipt of most of the proceeds. His state ceremonial, and the customs of the country, have been elaborately described by the missionaries, but they are too lengthy for us to recount. In the past there was much cruel human sacrifice and cannibalism among these people. Recently, fresh Catholic and other missions have gone to San Salvador, as the Portuguese call the Congo capital, Ambassi. Don Pedro, the present negro king, has become the vassal of Portugal; and French, Portuguese, and Dutch factories have been founded near the royal abode.

But the capacity of the Bantu peoples in this region for organisation is shown by various other tribes. In the region of the great river Kassai, a tributary of **Other Bantu kingdoms.** the Congo, the Walunda have an important kingdom (Ulunda), the king of which is officially termed Muatu-Yamvo. Another large kingdom near the sources of the Luapula, is that of Muata Kazembe. South of the Lualaba, or Congo, at Nyangwe, is the extensive kingdom of Urua, ruled by Kasongo, who appoints a large number of tribal chiefs, and maintains both a sort of feudal and a caste system. This kingdom is, in its turn, being cut down by the enterprise of the Kioko, a notable hunting race, including many capable smiths, who are gradually pushing northwards.

It is evident that the Bantu peoples of South Africa have an organising power formerly little dreamt of; and, like the Mahometan kingdoms of the Soudan, they give a very different impression of African character from that formerly derived from West African tribes and negro slaves in America.

It is very doubtful whether Europeans will do any good to the Africans by destroying those organisations among them which appear natural and suited to the people. To aid a natural development rather than to destroy it; to take advantage of such roots of sound growth as appear to exist, to supply means of civilisation in such directions as the Africans can appreciate; and to gradually introduce the elements of morality without asperity, and by means of example as well as precept, would seem to be the wisest methods. And it does not follow that Mahometanism should be regarded as entirely hateful or objectionable in Africa, if it will bind together peoples, teach belief in one God, and restrain the growth of intemperance, which is one of the worst contributions of Europe to Africa.

CHAPTER X.
The Malagasy.

Early inhabitants—European invaders—Radama I.—Ranavalona I.—Rev. W. Ellis—Radama II.—Rasoherina—Ranavalona II.—The French treaty—The Sakalavas—Primitive mode of burial—Religion—The Eastern coast tribes—The Sihanaka—A Bara warrior—The Hovas—Character—The Betsileo—Treatment of old and young—Houses—Handicrafts—Grades of rank—Laws—Religion and education—Former religious ideas—Mauritius and Reunion.

HOVA.

AT what period the great island of Madagascar became known in Northern Africa or in Asia is doubtful, but Early it is probable inhabitants. that Arab traders long ago voyaged thither. It was Marco Polo who made it first known in Europe, in the thirteenth century. Who were the original inhabitants of the island is quite unknown, but there are reports of former people allied to the Bushmen of South Africa; and considerable remains of early inhabitants who built cairns and tumuli and stone circles are yet to be seen. The vast proportion of the present inhabitants are undoubtedly descendants of invaders and settlers. Some of these are negroes from Africa, others are Arabs, others again are Hindus; but the bulk are of the Malay race, and all speak a Malay language.

Voyagers from Portugal discovered Madagascar in 1506, and named it St. Lawrence's island: in 1540 they at-
European invaders. tempted to settle there, but were promptly massacred by the natives, only a few escaping. Successive attempts of the Dutch and English failed; and in 1642, the French Société de l'Orient, under Richelieu's patronage, attempted to found a colony in the South-east; but the colonists endured many hardships and had little success for long, the chief result of their labours being the conferring of the name "Ile Dauphine" upon the island in 1665. Finally the French were driven out by the natives in 1672; but they never ceased to regard Madagascar as part of their dominions. In the eighteenth century repeated expeditions were sent thither from France, and a great deal of scientific exploration was done by French naturalists.

Probably the entire island has never been under one sovereign; but the Hovas have long been an important
Radama I. race and held extensive sway in the central parts. Long lists of their rulers exist. In the last quarter of the last century a chief succeeded, named Andrianimpoina, who, after adding several provinces to his territories, which still remained tributary to the Sakalava chiefs of Menabé, on the western side of the island, left his power to his son Radama I. (1810), who changed the face of Malagasy history. English soldiers were at once taken into his service to drill his army; treaties were made with the British; the Sakalavas were subdued; European missionaries were admitted and pro-tected; the foreign slave-trade was suppressed; schools were established; printing was introduced; and the French were opposed and attacked whenever they appeared. In 1828, Radama died and was succeeded by one of his
Ranavalona I. queens, Ranavalona, in consequence of a court conspiracy; and as her party were idol-wor-shippers, a reaction towards heathendom took place. At

first missionaries were tolerated, but after a time they and all converts were persecuted, a large number being put to death; at the same time anarchy prevailed in

many parts. For many years little intelligence about the Hovas reached the outer world, and it is only known that wars of a disastrous character were continually going on.

The Hovas continually attacked the Sakalava chiefs of the North-west coast, and the latter at last sought the help of the French (1839–40), who again made settlements. For some years the only European resident at the Hova capital was a Frenchman named Laborde, who was in high favour at court, and used all his influence in favour of the French.

In 1853, the Rev. W. Ellis, of the London Missionary Society, landed at Tamatave, and succeeded in reopening
Rev. W. Ellis. Madagascar to British influence. Meanwhile the crown prince Rakoto, son of Ranavalona, formally sought a French protectorate. After some daring attempts had been made by the Frenchman Lambert to effect a revolution in favour of the French, Ranavalona
Radama II. died in 1861, and her son (Rakoto) Radama II. became king. He at once proclaimed religious freedom, invited traders from Mauritius and Reunion, abolished duties on exports and imports, restored to their former owners lands which had been confiscated owing to their profession of Christianity, and in many ways showed a reforming spirit. He proceeded, however, too rapidly and offended too many prejudices, and he was
Rasoherina. put to death in 1863. His successor, Queen Rasoherina, was proclaimed; but the prime minister announced that "for the future the word of the sovereign alone was not to be-law, but the sovereign, the nobles, and the heads of the people were to unite in making the laws." Religion remained free, and friendship with foreigners was to be maintained; but the first article of the constitution was rather a startling one, "The sovereign shall not drink spirituous liquors." This reign was attended by continued sanguinary contests with the Sakalavas. Queen Rasoherina died in 1868, and the government proclaimed her cousin Ranavalona II. queen.

Her accession was marked by the non-bringing-forth of idols at her first public appearance, or at the funeral
Ranava- of the late queen. Christianity was at once
lona II. seen to have a stronger-hold upon the country. At the queen's coronation a copy of the Scriptures in Malagasy was placed by her side. The queen soon married

TRAVELLING ACROSS THE MOUNTAINS IN ·MADAGASCAR.

her prime minister, Rainilaiarivony. This was followed by the abolition of the privileges of the idol-keepers, and by the burning of the royal 'idols, an example which was imitated very largely throughout the country. Since then a general development of Malagasy power has taken place. In 1877, all the Mozambique (negro) slaves in the island were emancipated. In 1879, a responsible ministry was formed. In 1883, Ranavalona II. died, and was succeeded by the third queen of that name. We cannot give details of the recent conflict of France with Madagascar. Although the French may consider that they have gained something by their expedition and negotia-

The French Treaty. tions, their path was by no means easy, and the Hovas demonstrated that no power could readily overcome the difficulties of conquering them. The treaty of peace which the two powers signed towards the end of 1885, did not formally recognise the sovereignty of the Queen of Madagascar over the whole island; but her administration of the whole island is definitely mentioned. Even the French protectorate of the island, which was so vigorously claimed, is not granted, although the French are to take charge of foreign relations, through a resident at Antananarivo.

The Malagasy may be divided into, (1), the lowland or coast tribes, the Sakalava on the West, and the Betsimi-

The Sakalavas. saraka on the East; (2), the forest tribes, the Sihanaka, the Tanala, and Tankay; (3), the highlanders, the Hovas and Betsileo. The Sakalavas were until about two hundred years ago divided into very many tribes, but became consolidated into a southern (Menabé) and a northern kingdom (Iboina), having been united by the chiefs of a small tribe of superior energy, the Sakalavas. Until the rise of the Hovas in the present century, they were the most powerful people in the island, having European arms and ammunition, and apparently some European blood in the veins of their chiefs. They are as yet comparatively little known by foreigners, and missionaries have made little headway with them, as they are very superstitious. They are chiefly a pastoral people, and feed largely upon maize and other roots.

All the coast people are darker than the highlanders; but the southern Sakalava approach a negro complexion, and are of a strong constitution and fine physique. Mr. Walen, a Norwegian missionary, says : " They have long curly hair, high and broad foreheads, large and deep-set eyes, and wide nostrils, with supercilious airs and bold appearance, having good mental power and easily excited passions, making them rude, wild, and often raging in their conduct. On the whole, the Sakalava are a sly, perfidious, brutal, and arrogant people, given to stealing, drinking, fighting, and plundering at every place where they make their appearance." An European is never safe among them. They live in perpetual fear and suspicion of each other. Nobody is sure that his nearest relations are not plotting to kill him for his property, or to sell

HOVAS.

him into slavery. Fighting is a daily habit with them; but fewer are killed than might be expected, as they are not truly courageous. The coast people are largely fishermen, those a little way inland are husbandmen, the latter supplying rice to the former in exchange for salt and fish. The coast people have become considerably intermixed with foreign blood, Arab and negro. The southern Sakalava are very hostile to the Hovas.

The Northern tribe of the Antankarana, numbering not more than 20,000, retain many primitive beliefs and customs. The Western members of the tribe have embraced Mahometanism; but it has not a very great hold

Primitive mode of burial. on them. However, they shave the head and wear the long flowing dress of the Arabs. Their funeral ceremonies are old survivals. The corpse is sewn up in an ox-hide, and bound tight with cords. Then great quantities of beef and rum are consumed by the mourners. The cords are drawn tighter every day until only the bones remain. These are then laid in one of their long narrow canoes, with its two ends cut off square, and covered in, and the whole conveyed to the family cemetery on the east coast, amid continuous musket-firing. A cup and a plate are placed beside the coffin, and at intervals the friends go in large numbers and hold a feast of rice and rum in their cemeteries, where they are supposed to be joined by the spirits of their dead ancestors.

The eastern Antankarana retain their primitive paganism, but acknowledge one supreme God, whose presence

Religion. is especially associated with tall trees, high hills, and striking natural objects; and these are held sacred by them. Ghosts are believed to work all evil; and they have to be appeased, especially at places where any misfortune or accident has happened. They have a few priests,—a close caste, bitterly opposed to Christianity,—who are supposed to perform miracles, and bless or curse people.

The eastern coast tribes, of whom the Betsimisaraka are the lightest, with the straightest hair, are on the whole

The eastern coast tribes. much more gentle and docile than those on the West, and have submitted more readily to the Hovas. The more southern people are darker, and many of these have frizzly hair. They are not elevated in morals, and very idle, but are cleaner in their dress and dwellings than other tribes.

The Sihanaka live in the northern lake country, and are not very different from the Hovas, but much more

The Sihanaka. primitive. They have many cattle, grow much rice, and catch fish. The men fish for eels, the women catch small fish in a sieve-like basket, and the little children have their tiny canoes, from which they fish with bait. Some of these people are greatly addicted to astrology, observing lucky and unlucky days. If a stranger comes to them in an unlucky month, or day, or part of a day, they will not allow him to enter their village. Their houses are made chiefly of a plant named Zozoro (a tall sedge), the floor and walls being lined with fine matting. There are no partitions; the hearth is at the south-west, the bedstead (fixed) is at the south-east corner, with the head to the north, and between the hearth and the bedstead the master of the house has his seat. These positions are the contrary of those obtaining among the Hovas. Shelving is arranged all round the house, furnished with covered baskets and earthern dishes, made by the mistress and her female slaves. The men wear a cloth round the loins, and the end is thrown over the shoulders; the women wear a kind of skirt, which consists of a piece of cloth sewn up, into which they get like getting into a bag.

The Tankay, or Bezanozano, live in a very wooded country, with little open space for rice-growing. Both men and women plait their hair into very numerous long, narrow plaits, which hang loose about the head like a fringe. The Tanala inhabit a long stretch of forest region only a few miles wide, to the east of the central plateau and south of the Tankay. Some of their settlements, perched on lofty hills in the midst of forests, have never been conquered by the Hovas. The Bara, occupying an extensive country still farther south, are in a very uncivilised condition, divided into a number of petty States, constantly at war with each other. They are described as distrustful, suspicious, churlish and inhospitable, and very superstitious and immoral, being also very rough and filthy in speech and manners. The Rev. J. Richardson thus describes a Bara warrior: " His hair is done up into knobs of fat, wax, and whitening, numbering from ten to one hundred and twenty; and on the crown is a chignon of the same materials, about the size of, or larger than, a cricket ball; each knob is impacted against the other, and all have the ring of a hard wax ball. On his forehead or temples he carries his large

A Bara warrior.

charm, or round shell, about the size of a crown-piece. Round his neck he carries a number of beads of various sizes, and a few small wooden charms. In his ears he will have rings or pieces of wood, sometimes sticking in the lobe of the ear, and sometimes hanging down like ear-drops. Hanging round his neck, and resting on his breast, he carries a circular charm, about six inches long, covered with innumerable small beads, with two or more long ones at the end. The stock of his gun,—a flint-lock obtained from the traders on the coast,—is covered with brass-headed nails. His spear-heads are very bright and well-tempered. His belt, which is sometimes six inches broad, his powder-horn, his cartridge-box and tinder-flask, are decorated with brass-headed nails, to the number of 120, and each one the size of a shilling, or even a florin. Hanging from the shoulder and rest-

HOVA WOMAN.

ing on his right side, he carries his scarf of charms. Round his loins he wears a few yards of cloth, coloured or plain. Slung on his gun are a pair of sandals."

The Hovas of the highest stamp are comparatively few, and it has been conjectured that they are late immigrants from Java. They are of a light olive colour, although many of the people living with them are very dark, and are also called Hovas. They are mostly below middle height and well-proportioned; their features are rather flat; their lips are sometimes thin, sometimes rather thick; their hair is soft, black, and mostly straight. Their eyes are usually hazel. In all their movements they are graceful and agile. Their language is unmistakably derived from the Malay, like that of most of the other tribes.

Altogether, the Hovas are marked by much greater ability for governing, organising, and united action than the other tribes. Yet there was a time, not so long ago, when they were despised and pro- *Character.* scribed. No doubt they have cruel traits in their character, and have not unfrequently proved treacherous; but the influence of Christianity upon them seems to have been remarkably beneficial.

The Betsileo are a taller race than the Hovas, and several degrees darker; they evidently show traces of mixture with negro blood. Morally Mr. Shaw *The Betsileo.* described them as being in advance of the Hovas; but lying and cheating were not thought wrong. They are naturally a most quarrelsome and plundering people, and have very many slaves. They also spend much time in lawsuits, often, it is said, beggaring their families for the sake of a rice-field worth not more than eighteenpence. Drunkenness is very rife among them, rum being largely made. Their chief possessions consist of cattle; their wants are simple, and their habits indolent.

The clannish feeling is very strong among the Betsileo, the various tribes keeping themselves strictly apart. Family feeling is at the same time vigorous; *Treatment of old and young.* the young and old are well cared for. Mr. Shaw describes the love of the parents to their children as intense, and it is by no means uncommon to see the son carrying the aged parent on his back. They are really very hospitable, and owing to this have not unfrequently been imposed upon by strangers, who have stolen their children for slaves. They are fond of spending freely at funeral feasts and in providing large tombs for the dead.

The Betsileo appear to be scarcely, if at all, inferior in intellect to the Hovas, though they have not progressed

so far. The children learn readily, and take eagerly to
Houses. calculation. Many superstitions remain among
them, but Christianity is gaining ground.
Their small wooden or bamboo houses are so plastered
as to prevent ventilation, and the one door and one window are each not more than about thirty inches high and
a corresponding distance from the ground. The bedstead, reaching from the ceiling to the floor, is panelled
and closed all round, except a small opening. There is
no exit for the smoke, except by the window or door, and
all cooking is done within the house.

The Malagasy are very skilful in handicrafts. They
have long been expert at the manufacture of cotton, cloth,
Handicrafts. linen, and silk. Good cloth is made from banana
fibre, the rofia palm, etc. ; but these are mostly
now superseded by foreign manufactured articles. Mats
and baskets are very successfully made. A number of
industries connected with the hides and carcases of cattle
have lately been introduced. Pottery is largely manufactured, but without ornament. A simple mode of
smelting iron is practised, and a good many articles of
iron are made. Turtle-catching, for the shells, is largely
practised by the Sakalavas. The Hovas cannot be said
to have invented a very high order of architecture. In
1861, Antananarivo was crowded with wooden buildings
with high-pitched roofs and projecting horns; the roofs
were rush-thatched. There is seldom any ornamental
carving in these houses. In recent years, many brick
and stone houses have been built, and many artisan trades
have developed on the European model. Progress is still
retarded by inferior means of communication, roads and
wheeled vehicles being rare, and most commodities having
to be conveyed along rough and often hilly tracks on the
shoulders of bearers.

The Hovas have several important grades of rank, and
attach great importance to etiquette. After the actual
Grades of royal family, rank the descendants of the eldest
rank. and second sons of Ralambo, the ancient head
of the dynasty, who form two considerable clans. The
nobles, ranking next, act as judges, and deliver royal

messages to the people in their general assembly, or Kabary. Marriages are only legal between members of the same caste. Most of the laws are somewhat peculiar, according to European ideas. Thus, " any person having five houses and upwards destroyed by fire in the town, shall pay three bullocks and three **Laws.** dollars to the sovereign ; no excuse can be admitted, and the three bullocks shall be killed for the people in the town. . . . Any person found guilty of stealing fowls, shall receive forty stripes and have his or her hair cut off." But on the whole they are praiseworthy, and exhibit a distinct originality. Many of the ministers and government officials of the present day have been trained in the native Baptist colleges.

In some respects the Christian Church of Madagascar is peculiar, not specially following any English model. The pastors and officers are chosen by the **Religion and** people, and there is a mixture of Presbyterian- **education.** ism and Independency. A system of national education has been established, extending over the central provinces, and already achieving considerable results. Compulsory education has also been proclaimed in the Betsileo country. The total population of Madagascar is estimated at from four to five millions.

The religious ideas of the Malagasy, when the Europeans first visited them, much resembled those of certain Melanesian peoples. Believing in a vague superior **Former** impersonal power, they held it to be a sort of **religious** helper to be invoked. The good and the evil **ideas.** genius in nature impersonated, thunder and lightning and earthquake were venerated, as also were deceased sovereigns. The ghosts of ancestors were also honoured and prayed to as guardians of their surviving friends. Amulets and charms were trusted in by each person and family. Crocodiles' teeth were most potent charms. Many kinds of images were treated as gods, supposed to be active for good and evil. The powerful idols were kept in houses, where they were questioned, their votaries supplying the answers, giving cures and charms, and revealing the future. These idols were kept in great seclusion, although not at all extraordinary, usually human figures not more than a foot long; but they were always carefully wrapped in scarlet cloth or velvet. They were appealed to when taking the oath of allegiance to the king, or when taking the ordeal of the tangena poison. On some occasions they were carried about to expel diseases, to give courage in war, to protect against lightning, etc. The keepers of the national idols were much honoured, being regarded as nobles, and invested with the power of life and death.

Mauritius, 550 miles east of Madagascar, discovered by the Portuguese in 1507, was uninhabited, and its present **Mauritius** population is entirely due to immigration since **and Réunion.** then. The Dutch, who took it in 1598, named it after their Prince Maurice; but they abandoned it in 1710, and the French took possession in 1715, and called it " Ile de France." One of the ablest governors, Labourdonnais, introduced the culture of the sugar-cane, and promoted cotton and indigo growing; other French governors introduced other important plants, and Mauritius became a valuable colony. In 1810 the English captured it, and retained it after the treaty of Paris ; but it is still largely a French colony in language and in feeling, retaining many of the old French laws. There is a considerable mixed English, French, and half-caste population, and a much larger and very mixed Oriental one, Hindu coolies numbering two-thirds of the whole. There are also many African Negroes, Malagasy, Singalese, Chinamen, Malays. They have not always been well-treated by the planters, and much discontent has consequently arisen. Réunion, or Bourbon, 115 miles south-west, belonging to France, has a population composed of much the same elements.

www.ingramcontent.com/pod-product-compliance
Lightning Source LLC
Chambersburg PA
CBHW022131050726
47590CB00002B/498